AMERICAN HISTORY IN
100 NUTSHELLS

Also by Tad Tuleja

FABULOUS FALLACIES

BEYOND THE BOTTOM LINE

CURIOUS CUSTOMS

MARVELOUS MONIKERS

FOREIGNISMS

THE CAT'S PAJAMAS

THE CATALOG OF LOST BOOKS

QUIRKY QUOTATIONS

AMERICAN
HISTORY
in 100
NUTSHELLS

Tad Tuleja

FAWCETT COLUMBINE
NEW YORK

For my father

THADDEUS V. TULEJA

through whose eyes I first saw
the terrible beauty of
the human tale

A Fawcett Columbine Book
Published by Ballantine Books
Copyright © 1992 by Tad Tuleja

Library of Congress Catalog Card Number: 91-90640
ISBN: 0-449-90346-X

Cover illustration by Ken Dewey
Text design by Beth Tondreau Design

Manufactured in the United States of America
First Edition: May 1992
10 9 8 7 6 5 4 3 2 1

Contents

Acknowledgments

Since this book is intended for the general public rather than the professional historian, it would be pedantic to burden its acknowledgments with printed references. The reader should not conclude from their absence that I am oblivious of my debt to other writers. But that debt, while considerable, is not a personal one, and since the writing of history is always personal, I ask indulgence to acknowledge here that handful of historians whose special passions have helped to shape and inspire my own.

First and foremost is the spirit-kinsman of Magellan the Navigator to whom a grateful son dedicates this volume. Memory being what it is, I can't be certain, but I *think* that the first time I heard my father describe Jan Sobieski's charge at Vienna was my moment of realization that history was more than dates.

Other teachers have given other gifts.

Virginia Matthews, who taught me world history in fifth grade, watered what would become a lifelong zest for trivia with her exuberant "Yes!" at my remembering the literal meaning of "Patagonia."

Barbara Steidle, who ran an enthusiastic and rigorous U.S. history class at Bound Brook High School, New Jersey, helped me see the whys, not just the whats, in the American pageant.

To Rutgers University's John Lenaghan, my appreciation for a brilliant introduction to that venerable though now-assailed subject, Western civilization.

To the twin eminences behind Yale's old History, the Arts,

and Letters program, I owe the understanding that a good historian respects his Terence: *Humani nil a me alienum puto.* L. P. Curtis and the late Joseph Curtiss, to their eternal credit, were teaching "holistically" a generation before it was fashionable.

At the University of Sussex, where I searched for America in the frothy wake of the 1960s, Thomas Bottomore and Marcus Cunliffe, in different but equally enriching ways, showed me how social thought and social practice work together.

More recently, my father-in-law, Claude Nolen, has restored my faith that "doing" history can embody, not merely record, the human spirit.

For a discerning and helpful reading of the book's manuscript, my thanks to Howard Miller of the University of Texas's history department.

Finally, thanks as always to Professor Nolen's daughter Andrée, who provides the smile, and a dadgummit spark, that open my eyes.

Introduction

American History in 100 Nutshells

Aficionados of the television program "Saturday Night Live" will remember Father Guido Sarducci, at whose undeservedly obscure One Minute University the French curriculum was "Bonjour" and the economics final was "Define supply and demand." *American History in 100 Nutshells* is based on a similar, though postgraduate, premise. It may not contain every phrase that ever hop-skip-and-jumped through your mind in American History 101, but it contains every one that spent a weekend there—which is more than enough, these days, to win at "Jeopardy!"

But you don't need to be a quiz-show contestant to profit from this view of our past. Consider the following scenarios:

✪ Your immensely attractive, charming, and intelligent blind date turns out to be an expert on nineteenth-century imperialism. Need you hang your head and look moronic? Not if you've had the foresight to purchase this guide. A quick browse through its index will point you to no fewer than three entries relating to your date's forte, and you will soon be dropping "Open Door" and "yellow journalism" with the best of them.

✪ You're accosted on the street by a Roving Reporter who wants to know your views on the Middle East crisis. The previous interviewee mumbles something lame about madmen and oil. You, thanks to this guide, are able to characterize U.S.

options there as a choice between presidential principles. "Do we endorse Mr. Jefferson's eschewal of entangling alliances or agree, with Mr. Wilson, that the world must be made safe for democracy?" When your comment appears in the paper, NBC gives you Tom Brokaw's job.

✪ At a gathering of baby boomers discussing the sixties, you're at a loss to contribute anything of interest until the conversation turns to Vietnam. Your friends all remember where they were when two U.S. Navy vessels were allegedly attacked in the Gulf of Tonkin. Thanks to this book, you're the only one who remembers the ships' names. (Stop scratching your head and turn to page 197.)

These scenarios are only a few of the many in which familiarity with *American History in 100 Nutshells* can help you win friends, influence national policy, and appear savvier on our great democratic experiment than the professor who gave you a B minus in AmHist 101 could have imagined. It presents, in one hundred easy-to-digest gobbets, all the basic trigger terms, catchphrases, and stirring slogans that have actually, if truth be told, *made* our history, and through which that history is rightly remembered. With this book under your belt, you can bob and weave with anybody but Daniel Boorstin.

There are those who will quibble with my choices. I can hear the corner of the room sniggering now. "He only gives us 750 words on Manifest Destiny, can you imagine? Doesn't even *mention* the Whiskey Rebellion."

Not even true, by the way. You'll find the Whiskey Rebellion on page 41. And I'll tell you why the entries in this book are so short. It's because 750 words is 726 words more than the average college graduate could tell you about Manifest Destiny right now if you put a gun to his head and said, "Keep talking." Nobody remembers *anything* about the Whiskey Rebellion. This book is designed to help you "get along" in American history, so there's no point in loading it down with pedants' ephemera. Take it from a former Roving Reporter: Anybody who asks your views on the Whiskey Rebellion, you probably don't want to hang out with anyway.

Let me make it clear whom I had in mind when I wrote these hundred "nutshells." This book is for the average, reasonably literate American (or America-watcher) who recalls the phrase "Tariff of Abominations" but can't remember why it was abominable. Who *thinks* "Go West, young man" was Horace Greeley's line but wouldn't bet the ranch on it. Who's heard of Black Tuesday and Black Friday but isn't certain how they differ from your average blue Monday. Who, in short, once knew the phrases in this book and could use a gentle, and occasionally humorous, reminder of where they came from.

By my rough calculation, the people who fall into this "savvy but foggy on the details" category constitute 94 percent of the American population. The other 6 percent is about evenly divided between folks who agree with Henry Ford that history is "bunk" and academics whose idea of a good time is memorizing the names, dates, and favorite foods of the vice-presidents. If none of *them* buys this book, I'll sleep easier.

To the rest of you, a hearty welcome and these tips. The entries are arranged chronologically, so that if you really wanted to, you *could* read this thing front to back. There's a copious index, covering scores of phrases that didn't get their own entry numbers, as well as broad themes such as "Isolationism" and "Civil Rights." At the end of the main text I've thrown in appendices on campaign slogans, battlefield *bons mots*, and a selection of "gobbets" that I call, with an eye to pedant-deflation, the Dirty Dozen. This should be enough to help you parry most triviaphiles, although I'll admit it up front: Get cornered by a Whiskey Rebellion fan and you're on your own.

Tad Tuleja
Austin, TX

AMERICAN HISTORY IN
100 NUTSHELLS

"America"

Martin Waldseemüller, 1507

American history proper begins on October 12, 1492, when a Genoan sailor named Cristoforo Colombo, leading the vessels *Niña*, *Pinta*, and *Santa Maria* in a search for the spice-rich East, sets foot on the white sands of San Salvador. When Columbus went to his Maker, in 1506, he was still convinced that the land he claimed for the Spanish Crown that day was the fabled "Indies" his royal patrons, King Ferdinand and Queen Isabella, had sent him to find. Even though his error persists in the misdesignation of the continent's original inhabitants as "Indians," it was recognized as false as early as the sixteenth century. That's because a Florentine navigator named Amerigo Vespucci sailed west a few years after Columbus, saw the American landmass for what it was—a new world—and lent it his name.

Vespucci has gotten a lot of guff over the years for "stealing" Columbus's continent. I've had people who didn't know a sextant from a sexologist tell me that he was a lousy navigator, that he falsified records—even that he never made it across the Atlantic. In fact, the Florentine was so highly regarded as a navigator that he became Spain's pilot major and master cartographer. As for his journeys, although there is some question about how many times he actually crossed the Atlantic, solid evidence exists for at least two trips to what is now South America. After one of Vespucci's journeys, German cartographer Martin Waldseemüller published the first map of the New World *as* a new world—showing the southern continent as "discovered by Amerigo" and suggesting that the transatlantic lands be called "America."

Waldseemüller's claim for Vespucci's primacy was disputable, since Columbus had made landfall on South America in 1497. But of course the Columbophiles' "discovery" claim was also false. Good evidence points to a Norse discovery around the year 1000, and less widely accepted evidence suggests a fifth-century voyage by the Irish monk Brendan. This doesn't even take into account the Asian nomads who crossed the frozen Bering Strait in paleolithic times—those ancestors of Columbus's "Indians" whom historians Morison and Commager nicely call "our Mongoloid pilgrim fathers." In fact, if primacy were to determine the naming of the New World, it might better be called New Mongolia.

None of this, of course, diminishes Columbus's courage, his doggedness in the pursuit of his dream, or his phenomenal ambition. Nor does it deny the impact that his voyages had on the cultures of both Europe and the Americas. It has been said, quite rightly, that the admiral's landfall in the bright Caribbean that October day was "the most stunning accident in world history."

TIDBITS: ✪ *Contrary to popular belief, Columbus was not alone in believing the Earth to be a sphere; his specialness was in so underestimating its circumference that his patrons believed he could sail around it without running out of food. (And if America hadn't gotten in the way, that's probably what would have happened.)* ✪ *Other business, 1492: The capture of Grenada by the Spanish crown ends Moorish dominion in the peninsula; in the same year, Spanish Jews are expelled.*

"He That Will Not Work Shall Not Eat."

Captain John Smith, 1609

Most Americans remember John Smith as the luckless adventurer who is about to be brained to death by Powhatan's warriors when he is rescued by the chief's daughter, Pocahontas. The image is odd on two counts. One, it recalls an event that may not have happened. Smith was a notorious embellisher of legends—his own included—and historians are not certain that the tableau took place as he described it. Second, the tale paints Smith as a passive victim—as stumbling into an ambush and needing someone else to save his bacon. If it happened this way, it was hardly characteristic of the man. Tough, resourceful, and commanding, Smith did more than any other Jamestown settler to save the precariously placed colony from going under.

Jamestown, you may recall, was the second attempt by the English to settle the southern seaboard. The first, financed by Sir Walter Raleigh in 1585, was the ill-fated "Lost Colony" of Roanoke, whose inhabitants—including the New World's first English infant, Virginia Dare—mysteriously vanished shortly after its foundation. Jamestown fared better, and this was due in no small part to John Smith. The London-based Virginia Company, which was responsible for sending out the Jamestown settlers in 1607, wanted them to return the favor by seeking gold. The settlers proved so sedulous in this purpose that they neglected more mundane matters, such as hunting and planting, and after two years in Virginia were still struggling to fend off starvation.

Enter Smith, made council president in 1609, with a decree that would have seemed common sense had gold fever not been affecting people's brains. Since labor was essential to the colony's survival, he said, you must do your share or go hungry. This "work or starve" idea, a kind of Protestant ethic with teeth, was Smith's unyielding first commandment. He also encouraged trade with the Indians, built defenses, and mapped the country. His benevolent dictatorship could not prevent the awful "starving time" of 1609, in which hundreds died, but it did hold the shattered colony together until a relief ship arrived the following spring.

As for Pocahontas, she was also invaluable, with or without the legendary rescue. Smith, noting especially her gifts of corn, called her "the instrument to preserve this colony from death, famine, and utter confusion." She also had the good grace to marry Smith's fellow colonist John Rolfe, which helped reduce the friction between Powhatan's and Smith's people. An eight-year peace brought by their 1613 union enabled the colonists, under the entrepreneurial Rolfe's direction, to develop tobacco growing into a thriving industry—providing an acceptable substitute for the "Virginia gold" that was never found. From Rolfe's day up until the Revolution, tobacco was the principal cash crop of the southern colonies.

Over this happy enterprise, however, crept a shadow that would eventually sunder a nation. In 1619, a Dutch ship anchored in Jamestown harbor off-loaded twenty young Africans, brought in to harvest the fragrant leaves. Ironically, that same summer, the Virginia Company granted the colonists the right to convene an assembly of its own representatives. The resulting House of Burgesses, the first instrument of self-governance in the New World, was thus born, as historian Thomas Bailey poignantly phrased it, "in the same cradle with slavery."

TIDBITS: ✪ *Pocahontas was a nickname meaning "playful." Her given name was Matoaka. Christianized as "the Lady Rebecca Rolfe," she visited England in 1616 and died there of smallpox within a year.* ✪ *Many of Smith's contemporaries took up smoking in the belief that tobacco possessed medicinal qualities.*

James I, for whom the colony and the King James Bible were named, disagreed. In a famous diatribe against the "loathsome" custom, he likened tobacco fumes to "the horrible Stygian smoke of the pit that is bottomlesse." ✪ *Originator of Smith's "work or starve" phrasing: the Apostle Paul, in II Thessalonians 3:10.*

Mayflower Compact
November 11, 1620

The first settlers of New England were religious dissenters who came to be known as the Pilgrim Fathers. Disgusted with the rigidity and "Romish" vestiges (clerical vestments and holy pictures) of the English Church, one congregation of these Northamptonshire farmers left England in 1608 to seek a "purer" environment in Holland. Although they enjoyed religious freedom there for a decade, they became increasingly disenchanted with Dutch worldliness. In 1619 they approached the London-based Virginia Company—which had recently established the Jamestown colony—and asked to settle in the firm's northern territories. The resulting alliance was meant to benefit both the Pilgrims and their merchant supporters. The "Saints" (as they modestly called themselves) would be able to build a Bible-centered community; the Virginia Company would reap its rewards in the New World's abundant natural resources.

In September 1620, the Saints boarded the vessel *Mayflower* at Plymouth harbor and set their sights on the Western horizon. There were approximately 120 people on board, perhaps half of them Saints, the other half Anglican entrepreneurs whom the Pilgrims referred to as "Strangers." The inevitable tension between the two groups led to a document that is regarded, ironically, as the first evidence of civil concord in the colonies.

When the *Mayflower* sighted Cape Cod in November, it was obvious to the Pilgrim leaders that their business contract with the Virginia Company would, if they landed here, be invalid: the company's jurisdiction didn't reach this far north. This bothered the Strangers, too, who feared that without the company's ameliorating influence, the Saints themselves would become intolerant. Thus on November 11, as the ship rode at anchor, forty-one male members of the company put their marks on an impromptu "compact" designed to forestall future dissension by establishing the principle of consent to commonly agreed-upon laws.

The Mayflower Compact has been called everything from a consensus on majority rule to the New World's first constitution. Actually, it doesn't mention majority rule, and "constitution" comes in only as a future possibility. What the document did clearly establish was the concept of a "civil body politick" that would supersede the now-irrelevant Virginia charter; the notion that the signers would frame laws "for the generall good of ye Colonie"; and the promise of "due submission and obedience" to those laws. Not majority rule, then, but self-rule.

Armed with this paper bulwark against faction, the ship's company disembarked in December—an unverifiable tradition says at Plymouth Rock—and set about establishing a colony. That first winter they suffered under a "generall sickness" so severe that it carried away half of their number, but by spring, buildings were up, crops were in, and peaceful relations had been established with the Indians. One of them, an English-speaking Pawtuxet named Squanto, was so useful to the settlers (teaching them, for example, how to plant corn) that the colony's historian, William Bradford, called him a "speciall instrument sent of God." By the following October, the Pilgrims felt secure enough to hold a three-day feast for their Indian friends.

Tradition calls this event the First Thanksgiving.

In spite of their purist zeal and unworldliness, the Plymouth colonists achieved a reasonable degree of religious toleration and economic stability, relying on farming and a profitable fur trade. The colony's main achievement may have been the mere fact of its survival against stiff odds.

TIDBITS: ✪ *Squanto had previously learned English in England, where he lived for two years.* ✪ *Thanks to Henry Wadsworth Longfellow's poem "The Courtship of Miles Standish," the* Mayflower*'s most famous passengers were the captain himself, Priscilla Mullins, and John Alden. There's no basis for Longfellow's conjecture that they were principals in a love triangle.* ✪ *The prize for the weirdest names on the* Mayflower *goes to William Brewster's two sons, Love and Wrestling.*

Salem Witch Trials
Massachusetts Colony, 1692

That socially despised groups frequently become themselves intolerant is a sad reality of human nature. Seldom has this truth been more tragically displayed than in seventeenth-century Puritan Massachusetts. Fugitives from European religious intolerance, the Puritan elders established in the Bay Colony a prototype of theocratic inflexibility that strove to maintain the purity of its vision by expelling dissidents.

The most famous dissident, on both a political and a religious level, was Roger Williams. A clergyman with what were for the time strangely liberal opinions, he preached in the 1630s at Plymouth and Salem, maintaining not only that civil authorities had no jurisdiction over conscience, but also that they shouldn't steal Indian land. On both points he ran afoul of church elders, who banished him in 1635. His colony in exile, Rhode Island, became a haven for freethinkers of all stripes. A fellow Bay Colony "heretic," the inner-light preacher Anne Hutchinson, found refuge there in 1638. So did numerous Quakers, Jews, and forest "heathen."

A different kind of "dissidence" arose in the Puritan stronghold sixty years later. The power of the elders was then waning, and in 1689 Cotton Mather, third in a line of notable ministers, published a tract on witchcraft and possession, describing the trouble that the colony would be in for if it strayed from the Mather brand of Puritanism. Three years later, as if proving that the book was revelation, an outbreak of "witchcraft" engulfed Salem. It started when a group of teenage girls began behaving as if they were "possessed"—shaking, crying out for no reason, imagining strange torments and sexual fantasies. In the post-Freudian age, we have no difficulty seeing such behavior as hyperactive adolescentism, but in the seventeenth century it wasn't that simple. To Mather's readers, the girls were bewitched. A hunt for culprits promptly ensued.

The first "witch" to be found was a slave, Tituba, who confessed after being severely lashed. She named two other women as accomplices. At the urging of Cotton's father, Increase, a special court convened to investigate the girls' afflictions. Between May and October of 1692, the court found nineteen people guilty of witchcraft, and all were hanged. A twentieth victim, Giles Corey, refused to plead in his own defense; he was killed by being crushed beneath stones.

You might think all this would have pleased the Mathers, but they were rather less zealous than their followers. Both father and son repudiated the girls' "spectral evidence," Cotton counseled fasting and prayer rather than death for the accused, and Increase eventually stopped the trials by convincing the royal governor they had gone far enough. Four years later the jurors offered a public apology, and in 1714 the colonial legislature cleared the names of the score who had died for Salem's purity.

TIDBITS: ✪ *Cotton Mather, who wrote widely on both science and theology, was one of Yale College's founders and a defender of vaccination against smallpox thirty years before Edward Jenner was born.* ✪ *Notable modern treatment of this whole episode: Arthur Miller's drama* The Crucible.

French and Indian War
1755–63

The French and Indian War may have been the only war—certainly it was the most extended one—fought basically over a question of fashion. With beaver hats the rage in Europe, both France and England had set their sights not only on the wooded expanses of North America, but specifically on its fur-bearing animals. In fact, it was with the beaver in mind that the Virginia government in 1753 sent young George Washington to explore the Ohio Valley. The battles he fought with French troops there, at Fort Duquesne and Fort Necessity, were preliminary salvos for the war. He returned to the area under General Edward Braddock in 1755 as part of an attempt to reclaim the valley for the British. "Braddock's Defeat"—caused partly by the general's dismissal of Washington's warnings about ambush—was the redcoats' first major loss.

For the next eight years, fighting raged along the St. Lawrence River and in upstate New York. Because of the involvement of Indian allies on both sides, the conflict became known as the French and Indian War. The French, aided by their allies the Algonquins, won victories at Ticonderoga and Fort William Henry. The British, with the Algonquins' traditional enemies, the Iroquois, prevailed at Quebec and Montreal. After the latter city fell to the British in 1760, the war was effectively over, although the Treaty of Paris—which officially ended it—wasn't signed until 1763.

For America, the war had profound implications. Most important, the continent became British. In the Treaty of Paris, France surrendered all of known Canada (the Far West hadn't been explored yet) as well as all its holdings east of the Mississippi. Thus an enormous territory west of the Appalachians—rich in beaver skins, good soil, and (inconveniently) Indians—was opened up for English exploration. Second, the war gave young colonial officers like Washington their first taste of battle and frontier tactics. Third, and by no means least significant, the war strained the British budget to a breaking point. George II's government "won" by incurring a war debt of approximately 140 million pounds—which in those days was a tidy chunk of change. In addition, to defend its new acquisitions, it had to quarter, clothe, and feed garrisons of soldiers. It is by no means coincidental that two years after the ink dried at Paris, Prime Minister Grenville pushed through the Stamp Tax to pay for redcoat gruel in Massachusetts, setting the stage for an even more momentous conflict.

TIDBITS: ✪ *Three of James Fenimore Cooper's Leatherstocking tales*—The Deerslayer, The Pathfinder, *and* The Last of the Mohicans—*take place during the French and Indian War.* ✪ *Following a common practice of the time, General Braddock offered his troops scalp bounties, ranging from five pounds for a French soldier's hair to forty times that for a powerful Delaware chieftain's.* ✪ *Among the refugees created by the war were six thousand French-speaking inhabitants of Nova Scotia, or Acadia; sent to Louisiana by the British, they became known as 'Cadians and then Cajuns.*

"No Taxation Without Representation"

Prerevolutionary slogan

Throughout the seventeenth and eighteenth centuries, it was an article of economic faith that colonies existed to serve the mother country. Under the protectionist policy know as mercantilism, national power was thought to derive from a surplus of precious metals, and international trade controls ensured that the mother country got its due. Under mercantilism, colonies provided raw materials; the mother country turned these into goods and then sold them back to the colonies at a profit. Colonial trade with rival nations was discouraged by import taxes imposed by the mother country. But the colonies also profited under the mercantilist policy; they acquired protected markets for their native products and received bounties, or incentive subsidies, for certain items.

In British North America, the system worked well for a while. The colonists could send their tobacco to England's reliable market, and their concern about taxes was largely allayed by slack enforcement: the Molasses Act of 1733, which was supposed to keep French and Spanish sugar out of New England, was a paper tiger in the face of smuggling and wholesale bribery, and the region's rum industry prospered at the expense of the law.

What ended this scofflaw paradise was the French and Indian War. Overwhelmed with debts, Parliament made the ostensibly reasonable observation that the American colonies should chip in for their own defense—and started, for the first time in a hundred years, to put teeth into the import duty laws. In 1764 the Sugar Act strengthened the lax Molasses Act. The next year came the Stamp Act, which was to raise revenues for the garrisoning of troops in America by the sale of required excise stamps. The stamps provided the first real "direct tax" on the colonies, and they outraged merchants used to dodging the statutes.

Among the colonists' arguments against the new impositions was the idea that nobody should have to pay for the monetary support of a government in which he was not represented. This may sound like common sense today, but in the eighteenth century, few British subjects had their interests directly represented in Parliament; most were covered by the concept of "virtual representation"—the idea that Parliament indiscriminately spoke for "everyone." When Americans bucked this idea under the slogan "No taxation without representation," they were doing more than establishing the principle of direct representation; they were inching, ever so treasonably, toward popular democracy.

The concept of direct representation, if not the exact phrase, was probably first broached in a speech by the radical Boston lawyer James Otis. Denouncing the Stamp Act, he observed, "The very act of taxing exercised over those who are not represented, appears to be depriving them of one of their most essential rights; and if continued seems to be, in effect, an entire disfranchisement of every civil right." That was in 1765. Pressured, Parliament repealed the Stamp Act the following year, while simultaneously issuing the Declaratory Act, which reasserted its right to pass laws governing the colonies. A year after that came the notorious Townshend Acts, imposing further

duties on imports and leading to colonial resentment that culminated in the Boston Massacre.

TIDBITS: ✪ *The man who did mercantilism in: Adam Smith,
who published his laissez-faire classic,* The Wealth of Nations,
with wonderful serendipity, in 1776. ✪ *James Otis was said to
have expressed the wish that he leave this world "by a flash of
lightning." On May 23, 1783, he got his wish, when he was struck
and killed in an electrical storm.*

Boston Massacre

March 5, 1770

If Bostonians in the 1760s chafed at the very notion of taxation,
they were particularly incensed at the scarlet-coated troops
stationed within their town to ensure collection. The redcoats—"lobsterbacks," as the popular jibe had it—quickly became lightning rods for colonial resentment, and enjoyed about
as much support in old Boston as their descendants now find in
divided Belfast. The animosity between the soldiers and the
town came to a head on March 5, 1770.

The ground was covered in snow when the town bell
sounded a fire alarm, and the streets were soon filled with
curious youths, pitching snowballs at each other as they
searched for smoke. As it turned out, the bell was a false alarm,
but soon there was trouble enough of another kind. A crowd of
young men gathered in front of the despised Customs House
taunted and then pelted a British sentry. His comrades appeared in response to his calls for help, and scuffles ensued.

Shots were fired, and in minutes three Americans lay dead, among them a former slave named Crispus Attucks. (Two more shooting victims died later.)

That this brief, sad example of broken discipline should have become known—almost immediately—as a "massacre" was due in large part to Samuel Adams. Historian Carl Becker sums up his importance:

> No one, in the year 1770, was better fitted than Samuel Adams . . . to push the continent into a rebellion. Unlike most of his patriot friends, he had neither private business nor private profession to fall back upon when public affairs grew tame. . . . He had already achieved for himself the enviable position of known and named leader in every movement of opposition to royal or magisterial prerogative.

And no exploit was Adams able to turn to better and quicker advantage than that brief moment in front of the Customs House. Thanks largely to Adams's fulminations (and to an engraving Paul Revere circulated of the incident), the people of Boston were made acutely aware of the British soldiers' crime and brought several to trial (two were convicted of manslaughter). In a sense, fiery Sam's agitations had effected the first British "retreat" of the coming war, for the acting governor, Thomas Hutchinson, then withdrew the troops to an offshore island to avoid further entanglements.

As for the freedman who was killed, Crispus Attucks had fled from his Massachusetts master in 1750 to follow the call of the sea (not to mention liberty), and eyewitnesses to the events of March 5 said that he was the first to fall as a result of British fire. The soldiers, in defense, claimed he had attacked them "with malice aforethought." Scholars generally agree Attucks was mulatto—maybe Indian, maybe black, maybe both. As historian Benjamin Quarles says in the *Dictionary of American Negro Biography*, Attucks's obscure origins are ultimately less significant than his symbolic value for Americans of every color, in particular African Americans. A monument to Attucks stands on Boston Common.

T I D B I T S : ✪ *The British soldiers' defense attorney, who blamed Attucks's "mad behavior" for the carnage, was Boston lawyer John Adams.* ✪ *Before the Civil War, black army companies were often known as Attucks Guards.*

Boston Tea Party
December 16, 1773

Faced with colonial resistance to the Stamp Act, Britain's Parliament rescinded that measure in 1766, only to reassert its taxing prerogatives the very next year by passing the equally unpopular Townshend Acts. Named for exchequer chancellor Charles Townshend, these acts affirmed the Crown's right to quarter soldiers in the colonies; to levy duties on lead, paint, glass, paper, and tea; and to use the universally hated Writs of Assistance (royal search warrants) to uncover the whereabouts of smuggled goods. The colonials, as they had after the Stamp Act, resorted to boycotts and further smuggling to scotch the restrictions. The antagonism that the latest round of taxomania elicited culminated in the 1770 Boston Massacre.

Ironically, on the same day as the Massacre, George III's prime minister, Lord North, recommended the repeal of the Townshend duties—with the exception of the tax on tea. The irritation caused by that symbolic retention of parliamentary authority was exacerbated in 1773, when a new Tea Act gave the British East India Company a monopoly of the colonial tea market. Although that company had such a surplus of the leaves that the price to the colonists dropped dramatically despite importation fees, principle managed to outweigh monetary considerations, and throughout the colonies people still bought from the smugglers, refusing to be coerced into saving money.

Resistance came to a head in December, when 342 chests of East India tea lay waiting for off-loading from vessels in Boston harbor. Tea ships had been turned back before, but this time radical forces led by Samuel Adams opted for a more vivid symbolic action. Patriot clubs calling themselves "Sons of Liberty" had been active for almost a decade harassing tax collectors. On the night of the sixteenth they congregated along the quays dressed as Indians and, at a signal from Adams, dumped the waiting tea into the harbor. Copycat "tea parties" in other states soon followed.

Britain reacted by passing a series of acts that closed Boston harbor, subjected town meetings to gubernatorial approval, provided for the quartering of British troops in private homes, and immunized Crown officials from prosecution in colonial courts. The colonists dubbed these new restrictions the Intolerable Acts and quickly resolved not to tolerate them. Instead of capitulating, they convened two Continental Congresses in Philadelphia—the first steps in united resistance to British power. The First Congress, which met in the fall of 1774, made colonial grievances a matter of public record. The Second Congress, which first convened in the spring of 1775, had more far-ranging effects: It authorized an army, hired George Washington to lead it, issued money, and eventually adopted the Declaration of Independence.

TIDBITS: ✪ *The Maryland equivalent of the Boston outing was known as the "Peggy Stewart Tea Party," from the name of a tea ship burned by colonists.* ✪ *The American taste for coffee, according to legend, started on December 17, 1773. Not true.*

"Give Me Liberty or Give Me Death!"

Patrick Henry, 1775

Lucky for American legend, Patrick Henry had a poor head for business. By the age of twenty-four, this son of a Virginia planter had run two country stores into the ground, to say nothing of a three-hundred-acre farm. Realizing that his fortune might lie more in the realm of brain than of brawn, he applied himself to a study of the law and in 1760 was admitted to the bar. The country thus lost a piddling farmer but gained one of the most accomplished orators in its history.

In 1763, Henry defended a group of small farmers who, in accordance with a recently enacted Virginia law, had begun to pay their clergymen in cash rather than in the traditional (and more valuable) tobacco. Since the British Crown opposed this practice, Henry's stance showed him a strong supporter of colonial autonomy and made him a celebrity in the process. His impassioned attacks on clerical greed and royal intrusion made him the Clarence Darrow of his day.

Although Henry lost the case, he was then voted into the Virginia House of Burgesses. He took his seat on May 20, 1765. Only nine days later the freshman representative denounced the recently announced Stamp Act in words that resounded as far north as Boston. "Caesar had his Brutus," he declaimed, "Charles I his Cromwell, and George III . . ." Interrupted at this point by cries of "treason!" Henry waited for silence, and finished, ". . . and George III may profit from their example. If this be treason, make the most of it."

That zinger made him the leader of the Virginia radicals, and for the next decade he kept the banner flying. Elected to the first Continental Congress in 1774, he went to Philadelphia in September, speaking passionately in favor of boycotting British goods. Then, in March of the following year at a Richmond meeting of the Convention, came Henry's most famous line. With war obviously not far off, Henry called for an immediate "posture of defense." In the heated debate that followed, he denounced further conciliation in words that schoolchildren were forced to memorize for generations:

> Gentlemen may cry peace, peace, but there is no peace. The war is actually begun. The next gale that sweeps from the north will bring to our ears the clash of resounding arms. Our brethren are already in the field. Why stand we here idle? What is it the gentlemen wish? What would they have? Is life so dear, or peace so sweet, as to be purchased at the price of chains and slavery? Forbid it, Almighty God! I know not what course others may take. But as for me—give me liberty or give me death!

A superb orator or a world-class ham—depending on whom you read—Henry accompanied this ringing close with the extravagant gestures of a silent film star. On "chains and slavery" he crossed his wrists as if shackled, holding the pose to let the tension build. On "liberty" he flung his arms wide, and on "death" he stabbed his own breast with an invisible knife. It brought the house down.

When the "next gale" came, a month later, Henry put his money where his mouth was and organized the local militia. His wartime offices included those of governor and, briefly, colonial commander in chief. Still feisty after the war's conclusion, he became a major opponent of the proposed federal Constitution and championed the Bill of Rights as a check on its power.

Only in his last years did Henry falter in his opposition to Big Government—and this only because of a personal gripe. He and Thomas Jefferson, once friends, had fallen out in 1781 over Jefferson's management of the Virginia governorship, and the bitterness lasted for the rest of Henry's life. When the Jefferson faction was gaining strength in the late 1790s, Henry was persuaded to oppose them—which meant aligning himself, bizarrely enough, with the strong-government Federalists. In the spring of 1799, he actually won a Federalist seat in the state legislature. He died—perhaps of cognitive dissonance—before his term began.

TIDBITS: ✪ *Henry's famous option is preserved in the New Hampshire state motto: "Live Free or Die."* ✪ *Ironically, as a member of the postwar Virginia legislature, Henry fought for taxes far heavier than any that would have been imposed by the Stamp Act.* ✪ *George Washington offered Henry first the State cabinet post, then the chief justice spot; Henry turned both down.*

Paul Revere's Ride

April 18, 1775

Henry Wadsworth Longfellow had a fatal knack for enshrining history in one-liners, and several figures of American folklore come down to us filtered through his romantic lens. He gave us, for example, Priscilla Mullins's supposed retort to shy

John Alden ("Why don't you speak for yourself, John?") as well as the quaint notion that Hiawatha—actually an Iroquois statesman—spent his time mumbling endearments along "the shores of Gitchee Gumee." And it's because of Longfellow's poem "The Midnight Ride of Paul Revere" that most Americans believe the Boston silversmith warned the slumbering citizens of Concord, Massachusetts, that "the redcoats are coming."

In the spring of 1775, Revere and every other member of the anti-British Sons of Liberty were aware that King George's finest were about to move on American arms stores at Concord and arrest the rebel leaders Samuel Adams and John Hancock. Anticipating the move, Revere arranged for lamps to be lit in the steeple of Boston's North Church—"one if by land, and two if by sea"—to indicate the British approach. As Longfellow's Revere proclaims:

> I on the opposite shore will be,
> Ready to ride and spread the alarm
> Through every Middlesex village and farm
> For the country folk to be up and to arm.

The signal came on the night of April 18, and the patriot craftsman dutifully took his famous ride. What Longfellow doesn't mention is that he was aided by two other riders, William Dawes and Samuel Prescott; that Dawes and Revere were stopped by a British patrol and turned back; and that Prescott was the only one to reach Concord. Revere's main contribution to the night's business was to warn Hancock and Adams to get out of Lexington.

Aside from the difficulty of rhyming "Prescott" with anything but "waistcoat," Longfellow had a sound historical (or at least mythical) reason for favoring Revere over his fellow riders. Paul was not only a distinguished silversmith but a notable firebrand for the patriot cause. A major figure in the Sons of

Liberty, he published a drawing of the Boston Massacre in 1770 that helped to nourish colonial resentment of British troops, agitated widely against taxed tea in the early 1770s, and was one of the "Indians" at the Boston Tea Party. In choosing Revere over Prescott or Dawes, the poet was putting his money on a known winner.

TIDBITS: ✪ *A fine blend of artist and businessman, Revere was commissioned to print not only the first Continental money but also the official colonial seal. Plus, as a copper-sheeting specialist after the war, he was responsible for covering the dome of the Massachusetts State House and the hull of the U.S.S.* Constitution. ✪ *Nowhere in Longfellow's poem does the hero actually utter the words "the redcoats are coming."*

"The Shot Heard Round the World"
April 19, 1775

The shot referred to here is the volley fired by the Massachusetts minutemen who, on April 19, 1775, stopped a troop of British soldiers at Concord's North Bridge. Concord was a major supply depot, and on the previous day British commander Thomas Gage had sent seven hundred men toward the village to seize colonial arms. Militiamen first resisted them at Lexington, where they lost eight, and then at Concord, where they succeeded in turning the redcoats back to Boston. As battles go, it was small potatoes—the British lost seventy-three men, the Americans forty-nine—but it marked the beginning of military resistance by the colonies, and its repercussions were certainly felt "round the world."

Ralph Waldo Emerson coined the famous phrase in 1837, in the four-stanza poem "Concord Hymn," which was sung at the dedication of the Concord battle monument on July 4 of that year. The first stanza, cut into the stone, reads:

By the rude bridge that arched the flood,
Their flag to April's breeze unfurled,
Here once the embattled farmers stood
And fired the shot heard round the world.

In 1837, Emerson had just come into his own. After years of preaching, traveling, and lecturing, he settled down in Concord, where he wrote "The American Scholar," an essay that Oliver Wendell Holmes called the nation's "intellectual Declaration of Independence." In the 1830s and 1840s, Emerson associated with fellow New Englanders Henry David Thoreau, Margaret Fuller, and Bronson Alcott; the quasi-mystical idealism they promoted was commonly known as Transcendentalism. In essays such as "Self-Reliance" and "The Over-Soul," Emerson established himself as the intellectual voice of a generation, and he was in frequent demand as a lecturer on two continents.

Known for his richly styled prose, Emerson produced so many distinguished essays that he became known as the "sage of Concord." As for his verse, most of his stanzas sing the praises of Nature and of Nature's single, hidden "mind"; the topical, patriotic "Hymn" is an exception.

TIDBITS: ✪ *Emerson's 1838 address to the Harvard Divinity School put formal religion in such a bad light that his alma mater didn't invite him to speak again for twenty-eight years.* ✪ *Best Emerson takeoff: Gary Larson's cartoon of cows being loaded into a spacecraft, over the caption "The Herd Shot Round the World."*

"Yankee Doodle"

Revolutionary war song

Since this children's favorite has long been an unofficial national anthem, it's ironic that it started out as an anti-American tune, meant to ridicule the rustic ways of colonial soldiers. Legends of its origins vary, the most common being that it was penned by a British army doctor, Richard Shuckberg, to deride the motley "uniforms" of provincial troops stationed at Albany during the French and Indian War. (That was twenty years *before* the Revolution.)

Whoever wrote the song, it was widely sung in the 1750s and 1760s, and up until the Revolution it was still a joke *on* colonial forces rather than *by* them: a "doodle," in the eighteenth century, was a simpleton. Legend has it that what turned the tables was the Battle of Concord. British troops marched to the tune on their way to the fateful encounter at Concord Bridge; as they retreated from that first American victory, they had to endure "the simpletons'" fifes and drums picking up the air. The song soon became an American camp favorite.

Like any good folk song, "Yankee Doodle" grew by agglutination. By the time it first appeared in print in James Aird's *Scotch, English, Irish, and Foreign Airs* (1782), it had acquired dozens of verses. A character in the new nation's first native drama, Royall Tyler's *The Contrast* (1787), confesses that he knows "only" 199 stanzas. Today, although the tune's popularity has never dimmed, the first stanza is all anybody can remember. It goes like this:

> Yankee Doodle went to town riding on a pony,
> Stuck a feather in his cap and called it macaroni.
> Yankee Doodle, keep it up, Yankee Doodle dandy,
> Mind the music and the step and with the girls be handy.

The image of the dimwitted rustic, mistaking a feather for pasta, is a little misleading. In the eighteenth century a "macaroni" was a fancy dresser, or fop. "Handy" meant just what it means today.

"These Are the Times That Try Men's Souls."

Thomas Paine, 1776

Every so often somebody puts pen to paper and produces a document that actually, not just imaginatively, changes the world: Martin Luther's ninety-five Theses, which lit the match for the Protestant Reformation; Marx and Engels's *Communist Manifesto;* Stowe's *Uncle Tom's Cabin* (see page 83); and—more significantly than any other American document—Thomas Paine's pamphlet *Common Sense.* Published in January 1776, it did more than all the Sons of Liberty escapades and all the flourishes of radical speechmakers to make the American Revolution a fight for independence.

Paine was nearly forty when he wrote it, and up to that time he had achieved only an oddly dual reputation as an egomaniac and a failure. In his native England, he tried his hand first at corset-making (his father's trade) and then moved on, with similarly poor results, to shopkeeping and finally tax collecting. In this last position he organized his fellow underpaid excisemen, pled their case to an unresponsive Parliament, and wrote a pamphlet on their behalf. The pamphlet sank as quickly as Paine's fortunes, but it did get him noticed by Benjamin Franklin, who sent him to America to edit the *Pennsylvania Magazine*.

That was in 1774. Two years later, in *Common Sense*, Paine argued so forcefully against monarchy and in favor of separation from England that he became an overnight sensation. In denouncing "the corrupt influence of the Crown," he galvanized people who already hated George III; in urging his recently adopted country to become "an asylum for mankind," he prefigured Emma Lazarus (see page 114) by a century; and in defining the breach with England as "common sense," he both appealed to and redefined the spirit of Reason.

George Washington later observed that the pamphlet had "worked a powerful change in the minds of many men." Quite an understatement. It hit the streets with the punch of a Stephen King blockbuster. In the first three months alone, approximately 120,000 copies were sold, at a time when the colonial population (excluding slaves, who couldn't read) was less than 2.5 million. That's one in twenty people reading Paine.

The following year, he had another hit. With Washington's ragtag army having been pushed across New Jersey by the British, and with both hunger and desertions threatening the cause, Paine was asked by the commander in chief to produce something encouraging for the troops. He came up with the first of sixteen *Crisis* papers, read to the assembled Continentals on December 23. This essay begins with Paine's single most famous line, "These are the times that try men's souls," denounces the "summer soldier" and the "sunshine patriot" for lukewarm conviction, and defends liberty in words that would have tickled Adam Smith:

> What we obtain too cheap, we esteem too lightly; 'tis dearness only that gives everything its value. Heaven knows how to put a proper price upon its goods; and it would be strange indeed, if so celestial an article as freedom should not be highly rated.

Two days after hearing this, Washington's troops made their famous crossing of the Delaware and drove the British army out of Trenton. The Continental Congress rewarded the author by giving him a secretarial sinecure.

After the war, Paine returned to England, where his defense of the French Revolution, *The Rights of Man*, made such an impression on his former countrymen that they kicked him out. He went to Paris, got a seat in the National Assembly, fell out of favor when Robespierre came to power, was imprisoned for several months, and wrote a defense of deism called *The Age of Reason*. Widely viewed as atheistic, it didn't help his stock much in pious America. He moved back there in 1802 and died seven years later in New York City.

T I D B I T S : ✪ *Paine's most sympathetic biographer, Howard Fast, calls him "an exceptionally moderate drinker" for his time; most others suggest he could have gone one-on-one with William Faulkner and come up grinning.* ✪ *To attain the same proportionate initial success as* Common Sense *did in 1776, a book today would have to sell four million copies a month.*

"We Hold These Truths to Be Self-evident . . ."

Declaration of Independence, 1776

According to the epitaph he ordered, Thomas Jefferson wanted to be remembered for three things: founding the University of Virginia, drafting that state's act of religious toleration, and writing the Declaration of Independence. While we may wonder why he neglected to mention his presidency, the achievements he cited are not surprising. A well-bred and thoroughly Frenchified child of the Enlightenment, Jefferson dedicated his entire life to the pursuit of Reason, believing rationality and freedom to be the greatest riches of the human spirit.

Jefferson's legacy to Americans, his epitaph aside, *was* basically threefold. First, reflecting his Tidewater planter background, he articulated the myth of a New World agrarian paradise that has inspired the national imagination ever since. As suspicious of cities and industry as he was of autocracy, he painted farmers as the backbone of the nation, proclaiming with blunt piety that "those who labor in the earth are the chosen people of God." When historians speak of Jeffersonian democracy, they mean his vision of the sturdy yeoman as nature's nobleman. Jefferson's view brought him consistently into conflict with Alexander Hamilton, whose ideal America was a heavily industrialized merchant's paradise, where the central government actively supported business interests.

Jefferson's second contribution was states' rights—not a concept he had invented, to be sure, but one to which he gave the stamp of great authority. When the Federalist government in 1798 passed the Alien and Sedition Acts—a gag order prohibiting criticism of its policies—Jefferson responded by writing the Kentucky Resolutions, which proposed the supremacy of state over federal decisions. Here again he clashed with Hamilton, as the treasury chief was the nation's strongest spokesman for the central government's "implied" (and thus expandable) powers. Division among the Founders on this score led to Jefferson's victory in the 1800 presidential election as the head of a new party, the Democratic Republicans.

Jefferson's final gift—and one he himself recognized—was the document that defined the nation's guiding principles. When Richard Henry Lee told the Continental Congress in June 1776 that the colonies "are, and of right ought to be, free and independent," the delegates appointed a committee to put this down on parchment. As principal author, Jefferson strove not for originality (as he himself admitted), but for "the common sense of the subject," plainly stated. In this seemingly modest assessment of his duties, he was reflecting the Enlightenment's faith in human reason.

The bulk of the famous document, when finally approved a month later, was a list of grievances against the British Crown, ranging from the dissolution of colonial assemblies to the quartering of troops in private homes, from the imposition of taxes to the abolition of trial by jury. The broader brushstrokes of the document come at the end, where the colonies boldly declare their independence, and at the beginning, where Jefferson defines popular government.

He starts with the famous "when in the course of human events" preamble, saying in effect, "We're about to cut and run, so we'll tell you why." Then comes the most frequently, and justly so, quoted passage—Jefferson's beautifully phrased, reasoned defense of "self-evident truths":

> We hold these truths to be self-evident: That all men are created equal; that they are endowed by their Creator with certain unalienable rights; that among these are life, liberty,

and the pursuit of happiness; that, to secure these rights, governments are instituted among men, deriving their just powers from the consent of the governed; that whenever any form of government becomes destructive of these ends, it is the right of the people to alter or abolish it, and to institute new government, laying its foundations upon such principles, and organizing its powers in such form, as to them shall seem most likely to effect their safety and happiness.

In short, if your government isn't serving your needs, you can get rid of it and set up something else.

That idea might have been "self-evident" to Thomas Jefferson, but it was hardly commonplace to his contemporaries. Indeed, the historical importance of the American Revolution was that it tested these radical notions in the heat of battle. In this case, Continental might *made* them right. True, it took a Civil War to get blacks into the "all men" rubric, and another fifty years to break down the masculine bias, but Jefferson deserves credit for setting the model.

TIDBITS: ✪ *Congress only adopted the Declaration on July 4. The formal signing began two months later.* ✪ *At the signing, John Hancock remarked, "Now we must all hang together." Franklin added, "Or most assuredly we will all hang separately."*

"E Pluribus Unum"

Motto on the Great Seal of the United States

Among the "other business" that the Second Continental Congress addressed on July 4, 1776, was the appointment of a committee to design a seal that would become the official emblem of the United States. Committee members Ben Franklin, John Adams, and Thomas Jefferson initially suggested Biblical and mythological tableaux, but Congress said no good. It wasn't until 1782, with Cornwallis already beaten and peace negotiations under way, that the seal we know today was approved. It features, under a nimbus of thirteen stars, a spread eagle with its talons grasping arrows and an olive branch. The bird holds in its beak an unfurled banner inscribed with the Latin motto *E pluribus unum*—literally, "Out of many, one."

The design was new, but the motto went back to 1776: it was the only part of the trio's original suggestion that Congress retained. Franklin, Adams, and Jefferson had taken it directly from the legend of the popular *Gentleman's Magazine* and indirectly from a lyric by the poet Virgil. Whatever these sources meant by it, the current implication was clear. The new nation was to be a union of individual states. Perhaps, given John Adams's interest in a strong central government and Jefferson's countervailing advocacy of states' rights, the motto was the best compromise they could come up with.

The Great Seal's purpose was, of course, to *seal* things—specifically, to apply an embossed wax certification on U.S. treaties. To that end, physical seals have been kept in the State Department since 1782. The eagle has been "modernized" a few times since, though not recently: the design that you now see on the back of the one-dollar bill goes back to 1904. That's also true of the Great Seal's "reverse" design, the famous pyramid-plus-eye, which sits to the left of the "ONE." The Latin inscriptions above and below the pyramid mean, respectively, "He has furthered our endeavors" and "A new order of the ages."

TIDBITS: ✪ *Speaking of money, the English motto "In God we trust" was first used on American money in 1864; Congress made it the national motto in 1956—two years after deciding that the Pledge of Allegiance needed jazzing up with the proviso "under God."* ✪ *The bane of triskaidekaphobics, the Great Seal shows not only thirteen stars, but thirteen arrows, thirteen olives, thirteen olive leaves—and guess how many letters there are in E pluribus unum? ✪ Late-twentieth-century bumper sticker: "In God We Trust. All Others Pay Cash."*

"I Only Regret That I Have but One Life to Lose for My Country."

Nathan Hale, 1776

The American Revolution produced two noteworthy spies. The first, the worldly and artistic redcoat Major John Andre, was Benedict Arnold's accomplice in the plot to surrender West Point. Hanged on George Washington's order in October 1780, Andre was widely admired on both sides as gallant in death. A similar though belated adulation followed the British army's hanging of his American counterpart, Connecticut's "martyr-spy" Nathan Hale, now firmly implanted in American folklore.

A farmer's son, Hale was born in Connecticut, studied classics with the local minister, and in 1769 entered Yale College, where he shone both in the classroom and on the field. A shameless showoff, he was given to leaping over fences and in and out of barrels; in the words of the sober *Dictionary of American Biography*, "the marks of a prodigious broad jump which he made on the New Haven Green were long preserved." In spite of such saltatorial diversions, Hale managed to graduate thirteenth in a class of thirty-six and went to work in the fall of 1773 as a schoolmaster in nearby New London.

There he stayed until the outbreak of the Revolution, when

he—along with five of his eight brothers—resigned to join the army. As a Continental soldier, he seems to have been alert, resourceful, and dedicated with an almost Roman devotion to the good citizen's ideal of public service. He delivered a stirring call to arms after the Battle of Lexington, captured a British sloop in the spring of 1776, and during the New York campaign that fall, volunteered to go behind British lines to spy out their defenses. Hale's fellow officers urged him to stick to the uniform and to frontal attacks; Hale's reply was "I wish to be useful."

He was, almost. Carrying his Yale diploma to prove he was merely a schoolmaster, he spent two days scouting enemy entrenchments when the British found him and brought him to their chief, General William Howe. Since every martyr needs a Judas, it was believed that he was betrayed by his Tory cousin Samuel, but Howe didn't really need a finger man: Hale's "school" notes, written in Latin, included diagrams of defenses, and on top of that, he 'fessed up when they found him, proudly declaring his name, rank, and purpose. So much for the value of a Yale diploma.

This was on September 21. Promptly the next morning the young captain was hanged, but not before uttering a spirited farewell that closed with the fillip about his "only regret." A great line, but not original. Hale had lifted it from Joseph Addison's play *Cato*, in which the Roman statesman, mourning the loss of his patriot son, exclaims, "What pity is it, that we can die but once to serve our country."

T I D B I T S : ✪ *Both Andre and Hale hid their incriminating papers in their shoes—evidently an unbreakable, if foolish, rule of spy etiquette.* ✪ *Andre's words on his way to the scaffold: "It will be but a momentary pang."* ✪ *Killjoy historians claim Hale actually said, "It is the duty of every good soldier to obey the orders of his commander in chief." Give me a break.*

"First in War, First in Peace, and First in the Hearts of His Countrymen"

"Light Horse Harry" Lee, 1799

This panegyrical tribute has probably been applied to George Washington more frequently than any other phrase but "Father of His Country." Intoned at the first president's death by John Marshall, the phrase was actually invented by Washington's old army chum, Lieutenant Colonel Henry ("Light Horse Harry") Lee. It's got more than clever phrasing to recommend it, for Washington really was, to all but a small minority, the *numero uno* American of his time.

By "war," Lee meant of course the revolutionary war, in which he himself had served with distinction. Chosen commander in chief of the Continental Army in July 1775, Washington was faced with the formidable task of whipping a gaggle of ill-trained, undisciplined citizen soldiers into a force that could withstand the best army in the world. It took him a while, but he succeeded, besting the redcoats at Trenton, Princeton, Monmouth, and of course Yorktown, in the battle that ended the war. His ability to inspire his men through such ragged times as the 1777 winter at Valley Forge testifies to his leadership, and although that episode has been rosied up by legend (it's unlikely that Washington ever knelt in the snow, as the painting claims), contemporary accounts do agree that he was loved by his troops.

In peace, Washington's primacy was, if anything, more obvious. The former general was so beloved as the country's first president that he had to discourage designs to make him king. As chief executive he presided over not just the nation, but the organization of its first government. Congress created the first four cabinet posts, but it was Washington who filled them, making Thomas Jefferson secretary of state, Alexander Hamilton secretary of the treasury, Henry Knox secretary of war, and Edmund Randolph attorney general. He also chose the executive's first advisers, appointed judges, and in general established the patterns for things to come. As he himself once moaned, "I walk on untrodden ground. There is scarcely any part of my conduct that may not hereafter be drawn into precedent."

As for the hearts of his countrymen, he was pretty secure there too—but only after weathering a flurry of public enmity during his second administration. In 1794, a tax revolt by Pennsylvania farmers—the so-called Whiskey Rebellion—was quelled by federal troops (under Light Horse Harry), doing little to endear old George to backwoods voters. In the same year, he asked his chief justice, John Jay, to draft a treaty with a still-nettlesome mother country; because it overlooked such indignities as the impressment of U.S. sailors into British warships, Jay's treaty was denounced as conciliatory, and Washington was said to have "debauched" the infant nation. This was grave enough to make a third run at the office unattractive, but not so much as to prevent his quick resuscitation once he stepped aside. In the first generation after his death in 1799, he became a secular god to the American people.

TIDBITS: ✪ *Yes, he had false teeth. No, they weren't made out of wood.* ✪ *Revisionist historians and tabloid fans like to point out that he pined for his neighbor Sally Fairfax all his life, while being married to staid Martha Custis. So?* ✪ *Light Horse Harry's youngest son was Confederate General Robert E. Lee.*

"I Cannot Tell a Lie."

Mason Locke Weems, ca. 1800

It's arguably the most famous scene in American folklore. A little boy, hatchet in hand, faces his father. "Do you know who chopped down my cherry tree?" the elder asks. "I cannot tell a lie," answers the kid. "I did it with my trusty little hatchet." Whereupon old Dad, stricken with pride, embraces the boy, knowing that a truthful child is worth far more, in the Greater Scheme of Things, than whole ovens full of cherry pies.

Every schoolchild knows, even in these cliophobic times, that the lad here is young George Washington and that his confession was representative of his saintlike probity. The tableau is so well known that merchants advertise Presidents' Day sales with promises that they are "hacking" or "slashing" prices, and cartoon figures from Bugs Bunny to Elmer Fudd have made appearances with knee breeches and "widdle" hatchets.

Ironically, though, the story, and the line, are both fiction. They first appeared in Mason Locke Weems's *Life of Washington*, which came out shortly after the first president's death. Weems was a master at creating richly embroidered moral tales, and he was singularly unfussy about citing his sources. The hatchet tale, for example, came from an unnamed (and thus untraceable) "aged lady" who was supposed to have known Washington at Mount Vernon. The *National Enquirer* checks its facts better.

Weems was an Episcopal minister who, beginning in the 1790s, turned to bookselling not only to make a living, but to spread a gospel of moderation through the South. In partnership with a Philadelphia publisher, he spent decades hawking Bibles and other uplifting works at county fairs and backwoods commons, often lacing his sales pitches with impromptu sermons and, according to his biographer, Lewis Leary, "with occasional mild ribaldries to keep his listeners alert."

He wrote, too, producing a score of edifying volumes, ranging from pirated "revisions" of temperance tracts to lives of William Penn and Benjamin Franklin, and a smorgasbord of admonitions against indulgence, including such blockbusters as *The Drunkard's Looking Glass* and *God's Revenge against Adultery*. If Weems were alive today, he would write for Jimmy Swaggart.

In his excellent study of the nineteenth-century "Washington cult," historian Barry Schwartz argues that Washington's appeal to most Americans lay not in any real moral perfection, but in "his simultaneous inclination toward waywardness and repentance." "Self-mastery," Schwartz writes, "depends upon the recognition of one's own defects, and perhaps nothing better attests to America's regard for this attribute than the continuing popularity of the cherry tree story." What the cherry tree tale really shows, then, is not that the Father of His Country was flawless, but that he owned up to his mistakes and kept on trying.

TIDBITS: ✪ *The parson's name is pronounced "Wems," to rhyme with gems.* ✪ *In his version of the tale, the tree is not chopped down, but "barked so terribly, that I don't believe the tree ever got the better of it."* ✪ *The best gloss on the exemplum is still Mark Twain's. He claimed moral superiority to little George on the grounds that he* could *lie if he liked—but chose not to.*

"In Order to Form a More Perfect Union . . ."

Constitution of the United States, 1787

Even before the American colonists won their Revolution, they sought to define the structure of a common government that would make a fact of the symbolic credo *E pluribus unum* (see page 31). Their first attempt to do this was the Articles of Confederation, approved by the states in 1781. A noble experiment without much effectiveness, it left virtually all power in the hands of the individual states, making the Philadelphia "central" government a paper tiger. Most legislation, for example, required approval from nine of the thirteen states; amending the Articles themselves required unanimity. Congress lacked authority over taxation and international commerce; on other matters it could request or propose but had no power to enforce. Court decisions were entirely in state hands, and the executive branch of the government did not even exist.

The inherent weakness of this configuration became evident in 1786, when an army of veterans under Daniel Shays converged on Springfield, Massachusetts, to protest mortgage foreclosures. Although Shays's Rebellion failed in its aims, the rebels did manage to take over a federal armory and shake the equanimity of wealthy Americans who feared repeat performances of such debtors' resentment. The incident pointed up the need for a stronger federal government, and the following year a convention met to form one. Composed of only fifty-five delegates—all of them from the property-owning class—the convention met in Philadelphia, hammering out a slate of compromises that would replace the impotent Articles of Confederation.

"Compromise" is the right term, for the document Americans today consider sacrosanct was fought out, line by line, by competing parties. Of many compromises, consider only these five:

⊘ *"Large state" vs. "small state."* Should the states be represented in Congress on the basis of population or equally, as under the existing Articles? Populous Virginia pushed the former, "large state" plan, tiny New Jersey, with equal tendentiousness, the "small state" option. The compromise was to fashion a two-house Congress, with the upper house going New Jersey's route, the lower house Virginia's. Hence the Senate and the House of Representatives, respectively.

⊘ *Slave vs. free.* Should "all men," as the Declaration implied, be counted in apportioning taxes and representatives, or should slaves be considered less than "men"? The question, of course, ate its way like an insidious termite through the increasingly divided house of the subsequent century. For the moment, though, the Philadelphia delegates hit on this compromise: Each of the South's millions of slaves would count as three-fifths of a person.

⊘ *Direct or indirect election.* Should the president be elected directly by all the people—thus opening the way to mob rule and demagogy—or should more "qualified" people be chosen to make the decision? This question, which anticipated later conflict between the "well born" Federalists and the more broad-based Jeffersonians, was decided by the creation of the electoral college, whose members, chosen by the states, actually voted for the president. The system, which has irritated populists ever since, has also given us more than a dozen "minority presidents"—those elected with less than half the popular vote.

⊘ *Congress vs. the Executive.* Who should rule, the legislature or the president? To a people only recently escaped from monarchy, the answer might have seemed obvious, but in fact compromise figured in here, too. Congress was given the power to pass laws, while the president could only recommend them. The president, on the other hand, could veto Congress's wishes—unless they overrode his negation by a two-thirds majority.

★ *Federalists vs. states' rights.* Should the central government or the individual states be supreme? The "compromise" on this one was really a victory for Federalist delegates—people like James Madison and Alexander Hamilton, who favored a central government superior to that of the states and who therefore suggested that the new document be approved when endorsed by a mere two-thirds of the states' conventions. Anti-Federalists shrieked "foul" to no avail, and a hot spring of debate rapidly ensued, with Federalists pushing the strong-government line, and southern radicals, especially Patrick Henry, denouncing the document as a sellout of states' rights. In the end, the Federalists won, although the conflicting philosophies implicit in the debate have animated American history ever since.

A postlude came in the form of another "poor folks" rebellion. In 1794, farmers in western Pennsylvania revolted against a federal tax on whiskey, tarring and feathering revenue collectors and mounting the first dramatic challenge to the Constitution. President Washington responded by sending in thirteen thousand state militiamen (an enormous show of force for the time), who overpowered the rebels and pardoned the ringleaders. This short-lived Whiskey Rebellion thus provided a symbolic closing to the fear of federal impotence that had begun with Shays's Rebellion. The federal government might not be universally loved, but when it spoke, the people now would listen.

TIDBITS: ★ *Yes, the phrase "more perfect" is ungrammatical; even if you're James Madison, you shouldn't compare abso-*

lutes. ✪ *Most famous defense of the strong-government thesis:* The Federalist Papers, *by James Madison, Alexander Hamilton, and John Jay.* ✪ *Who selected the Constitutional Convention delegates? One-quarter of the country's white males.*

Northwest Ordinance
Organizing the "Old Northwest," 1787

Despite its general powerlessness, the central government under the Articles of Confederation did manage to pass one significant piece of legislation: the 1787 Northwest Ordinance. This pioneering land law established federal jurisdiction over the vast, unexplored "Old Northwest," which the new nation had acquired from Great Britain in the Revolution. Renamed the Northwest Territory, the area encompassed a quarter of a million square miles and eventually became the states of Ohio, Indiana, Illinois, Michigan, and Wisconsin. The Northwest Ordinance provided for the creation of these states and for their admission, on an equal footing with the original thirteen, into the Union.

According to the 1787 law, the Old Northwest would be administered initially by district officials appointed by the Congress. When population in any one of its several districts reached sixty thousand, the district could petition for statehood—with three to five states to be carved out of the region overall. Ohio came in first, in 1803, and the other four followed in due course. Since all of them lay to the west of Northern free states—in fact, the Northern states had ceded this land to the central government—it was not surprising that the Ordinance also prohibited slavery. Thus, in the 1780s, this divisive issue was already in evidence.

Land speculators bought up much of the newly available land, but individual farmers also moved in, and all clashed frequently with the native peoples who had lived there for centuries. The Ohio Valley had long been the site of red-against-white violence, and the new influx of settlers exacerbated the tension, leading to pitched battles between U.S. forces and indigenous tribes. The most famous of these battles took place at Fort Wayne (1791), Fallen Timbers (1794), Tippecanoe (1811), and the Thames (1813). At Fort Wayne, Miami Indians under Little Turtle routed soldiers under territorial governor Arthur St. Clair. As a result of General Anthony Wayne's victory at Fallen Timbers, the northern tribes surrendered their land and moved west. At Tippecanoe, Indiana territorial governor William Henry Harrison narrowly overcame the forces of a charismatic Shawnee leader called the Prophet, and at the Battle of the Thames he finally shattered the plans of the Prophet's brother, Tecumseh, for a grand alliance to end white encroachment.

TIDBITS: ✪ *Dates of admission to the Union: Indiana, 1816; Illinois, 1818; Michigan, 1837; Wisconsin, 1848.* ✪ *Tecumseh, who had participated in the 1791 victory against St. Clair, died of wounds received at the Battle of the Thames.* ✪ *Harrison's most famous, although not most decisive, victory gave him the nickname "Old Tippecanoe," on which he rode to the presidency in the 1840 election.*

Bill of Rights

Constitutional amendments, ratified 1791

Although the Constitution was finally ratified in 1790, one of the Anti-Federalists' chief complaints against it still remained: It lacked an individual bill of rights protecting citizens from potential government abuse. As Jefferson's Declaration made clear, independence had been sought to safeguard personal liberty. What he and other states'-righters most feared was that the U.S. government might copy the British and oppress its citizenry. To mollify them, champions of the Constitution agreed to add a bill of rights. The document's first ten amendments fulfilled that promise.

The First Amendment has generated as much controversy as any piece of writing in our history. It promises that Congress will legislate no "establishment of religion" and that it will honor the people's rights to free speech, assembly, and petition. In other words: any crackpot with working vocal cords can say whatever he wants on any subject. The American Civil Liberties Union has made defense of this amendment its raison d'être, and to liberals at large it's *the* American birthright. Conservatives are periodically peeved when it's used to ban public prayer, although they seem willing to recognize its utility when gag orders are imposed on "subversive" journalists. To liberals and conservatives alike, the street translation of the First Amendment is the solecism "Everybody has a right to his or her opinion."

The Second Amendment has also ruffled feathers. It secures "the right of the people to keep and bear arms." Although the Founders stipulated a reason for this guarantee—"a well-regulated militia being necessary to the security of a free State"—the National Rifle Association reads it as a blanket permission. Congressional attempts to regulate, or even register, firearms constantly fail before Second Amendment–waving shootists, who believe that since the Bill of Rights doesn't spell it out, there's no difference between a Saturday-night special and a deer gun.

The Third Amendment hasn't given much trouble. It prevents the government from quartering its soldiers in private homes except in wartime, and then only with the owner's permission. Serious business in the 1770s, you'll remember, but moot today.

Amendment Four *has* created problems, especially in these drug-laden times. A reflex against His Majesty's duty inspectors, it prohibits "unreasonable searches and seizures of persons and property," stipulating that even reasonable searches must be made on "probable cause." Watch any cop or lawyer show for ten minutes and you will realize this is not a dead issue. When the drug enforcement boys break into a crack house to arrest its inhabitants, either they have a search warrant and reasonable cause, or they lose the case because their evidence, although compelling, is inadmissible.

The Fifth and Sixth Amendments preserve the rights of accused persons to what we conventionally call "due process." The Fifth requires a grand jury for "infamous crimes," prohibits double jeopardy (being tried twice for the same crime), and allows a defendant to refuse to testify against himself. This last right was so abused by racketeers during the 1951 Senate investigations of organized crime that "taking the Fifth" became an American catchphrase.

The Sixth Amendment provides protection in criminal proceedings, specifically the rights to a "speedy and public" trial, to a jury, to come face-to-face with one's accusers, to "be informed of the nature and cause of the accusation," and to have the assistance of legal counsel. Check the cop shows again. When Joe Sleaze is collared two blocks from the scene of the crime, he is not simply thrown in the slammer. First the cops "read him his rights" (or "Mirandize" him), in a formula that paraphrases the Fifth and Sixth Amendments. As of 1966, when the Supreme Court issued its famous Miranda ruling, the police must do this or risk losing the suspect on a technicality.

The Seventh Amendment provides for trial by jury in civil suits where the value in dispute is more than twenty dollars. Today most of these cases are settled out of court, as it's more practical.

The Eighth Amendment proscribes "excessive" bail or fines as well as "cruel and unusual punishments." The definition of "excessive" is a matter of judicial discretion and seldom muddies the water of public debate. "Cruel and unusual" is another matter. Opponents of the death penalty use this amendment as their first line of attack on executions, and in 1972 they won a victory when the Supreme Court called for a reassessment of capital punishment. With the resurgence of death penalty statutes in the Reagan years, the Eighth Amendment was itself reassessed: lethal injection is now legally benign—and increasingly usual.

Amendments Nine and Ten speak directly to the Anti-Federalists' fear of a strong, potentially abusive central government. The Ninth, addressing "nonenumerated" rights, says that just because a right isn't mentioned in the Constitution doesn't mean it can be denied to the people. The Tenth, the flip side, says that any powers not expressly delegated to the feds "are reserved to the States respectively, or to the people." This wording is the principal bulwark of strict constructionism.

TIDBITS: ✪ *Nature lover's rewrite of the Second Amendment: "Preserve our right to arm bears."* ✪ *To "Mirandize" comes from Ernesto Miranda, the convicted rapist freed by the Supreme Court because he had not understood his rights when arrested.* ✪ *Other business, 1791: Alexander Hamilton founds the first U.S. national bank, realizing the strict constructionists' worst misgivings.*

"Millions for Defense, but Not One Cent for Tribute!"

Robert Harper, 1798

The Treaty of 1783, which ended the revolutionary war, got Great Britain off the colonists' backs in theory but not in fact. A decade later, the former mother country still maintained forts along the St. Lawrence River, continued to encourage Indian attacks on frontier settlers, and—since the outbreak of war with revolutionary France in 1793—had begun to interdict American ships carrying supplies to that country and its West Indian colonies. To prevent a resumption of hostilities, President Washington authorized his chief justice, John Jay, to draft a treaty by which England abandoned the forts and paid damages for seized ships and seamen—but made no promises about inciting the Indians or future seizures.

Jay's Treaty was so reviled in America that it contributed to Washington's decision not to seek a third term. It wasn't too popular in France, either. Not only did it implicitly repudiate the Franco-American Alliance of 1778, which had brought France into the Revolution against England, but it also allowed the French to believe, with some justice, that the United States had bought peace with England at her expense. In retaliation she sent *her* sailors against American ships, seizing hundreds and, following Britain's lead, abusing their crews.

To sort this mess out, President John Adams in 1797 sent two envoys, John Marshall and Elbridge Gerry, to assist ambassador Charles Pinckney in negotiating a solution. They were ungraciously received. Rather than dealing with the American trio directly, the French foreign minister, Talleyrand, sent three functionaries of his own to demand reassertion of the 1778 treaty and, incidentally, a quarter of a million dollars as a personal bribe. This was too much for America, which then recalled its envoys.

In its report to the president, the Pinckney legation identified Talleyrand's three messengers anonymously as ministers X, Y, and Z. Soon thereafter the incident became known as the "XYZ affair," and Americans clamored for war. The patriotic song "Hail, Columbia" ("Immortal patriots, rise once more/ Defend your rights, defend your shore") became the pick hit of the year. Fighting, which occurred exclusively at sea, lasted from 1798 to 1800.

It wasn't much of a war, as wars go—the books call it the "Undeclared War" or the "Quasi-War"—but it did give us one undying slogan. When Pinckney heard of Talleyrand's bribe demand, he burst out, "No, no, not a sixpence!" Although firm and to the point, this sounded more like a children's nursery rhyme than an ambassadorial pronouncement, so when Congressman Robert Harper of South Carolina toasted John Marshall in 1798 with the more authoritative line "Millions for defense, but not one cent for tribute," the papers promptly attributed it to Pinckney. Same idea, anyway.

TIDBITS: ✪ *Lasting outcomes of the XYZ war fever: the establishment of the Navy Department and the Marine Corps.* ✪ *Real names of the abecedarian trio: Bellamy, Hauteval, and Hottinguer.* ✪ *Nobody ever calls Talleyrand anything but Talleyrand—but in case anybody asks, his full name was Charles-Maurice de Talleyrand-Périgord, a.k.a. Prince de Bénévent.*

"Entangling Alliances with None"

Thomas Jefferson, 1801

The touchstone catchphrase of American isolationists throughout our history, this line appeared in the third President's first inaugural address, where he defined his foreign policy in twelve words: "peace, commerce, and honest friendship with all nations, entangling alliances with none." Neutrality had been a crucial element in Jefferson's attitude toward other nations ever since he was Washington's secretary of state, and his formulation of the doctrine rephrased a caution that Washington had uttered four years before, when in his farewell address he had warned against "permanent alliances with any portion of the foreign world."

Both Jefferson and Washington had reason to be suspicious of foreign ties. In 1778, in exchange for French support in the Revolution, the colonies had promised to defend French interests in the West Indies. Yet this promise became a liability when France and England went to war in 1793, and it contributed eventually to our "Quasi-War" with France. In addition, Washington was averse to mixing it up with the "embroiled" Europeans. The farewell address, while acknowledging the need to honor "existing engagements," simmers with contempt for "partiality" and "foreign influence":

> Europe has a set of primary interests which to us have none or a very remote relation. Hence she must be engaged in frequent controversies, the causes of which are essentially foreign to our concerns.... Why, by interweaving our destiny with that of any part of Europe, entangle our peace and pros-

perity in the toils of European ambition, rivalship, interest, humor, or caprice?

There wasn't a good reason, he concluded. Hence national interest meant keeping our distance, trusting only to "temporary alliances for extraordinary emergencies." Jefferson's catchphrase seconded that opinion.

As unrealistic as this opinion may seem in America today, it was by no means eccentric in 1801, or for a century thereafter. The United States conducted the War of 1812 without French aid; in 1823, the fifth President repackaged the nonalliance idea in his famous Monroe Doctrine (see page 57); and for seventy-five years after that, in spite of Manifest Destiny and a war with Mexico, America pretty much went along with Jefferson's advice. It wasn't until the Spanish-American War (see page 127) that American isolationism began to crumble, and even then such a fear of "involvement" hung on that it slowed our entry into both world wars.

Ubiquitous involvement is now fundamental to U.S. foreign policy. For that we can thank World War II and its cold war aftermath. When John F. Kennedy promised in 1961 that the United States would "go anywhere" and "pay any price" to secure liberty, you knew the Founding Fathers' warning was passé.

TIDBITS: ✪ *The contrary position, sharply stated by Harry Truman: "Isolationism is the road to war. Worse than that, isolationism is the road to defeat in war."* ✪ *Other business, 1801: the British government adopts the Union Jack.*

Lewis and Clark Expedition

1804–1806

In October 1803, the United States doubled its territory overnight by acquiring from France nearly the entire Great Plains between the Mississippi River and the Rocky Mountains. France herself had gotten this plum territory from Spain only two years before, and her ambitious ruler, Napoleon Bonaparte, had hoped to make it the heartland of a New World empire. To be in a sound strategic position to administer the territory, however, the Little Corporal had first to conquer Hispaniola, his intended base of operations in the Caribbean. His failure to do that, compounded by the need to raise funds for an anticipated war with Great Britain, led him to offer "Louisiana" to the Americans for the bargain-basement price of $15 million.

Thomas Jefferson, who was interested in the strategic port of New Orleans but had never dreamed about getting Kansas in the bargain, chewed his nails for six months before agreeing to the deal. A strict constructionist, he realized very well that the Constitution did not authorize him to make such a purchase. Thus he deliberated long and hard, until expansionists finally reminded him of Napoleon's volatility and made him realize that the deal was now or never.

Having secured this vast territory, Jefferson determined to find out what was in it. Accordingly he commissioned his former neighbor, Meriwether Lewis, and Lewis's former commanding officer, William Clark, to explore and report on the "soil and face of the country." If they happened upon a water route to the Pacific—the famous Northwest Passage that sailors had sought for three hundred years—so much the better.

Setting out from St. Louis, Lewis and Clark started, with forty-five men, up the Missouri River in May 1804. By the time they reached the Dakotas, they had put sixteen hundred miles behind them. After wintering among the Mandan Indians, they set out again the following April, accompanied by a French-Canadian interpreter, Toussaint Charbonneau, his teenage Shoshone wife, Sacajawea, and the couple's infant son, Jean Baptiste. Sacajawea's loyalty and language skills, not to mention her very presence, softened the belligerence of the northern tribes; one observer called her "time and again the genius of the occasion." In August the expedition crossed the Continental Divide, and in November it reached the Pacific. The following spring, they retraced the four-thousand-mile journey, returning to St. Louis in September 1806.

One of the great treks in history, Lewis and Clark's journey provided an enormous store of data about the American wilderness while serving as a probe for what was later called Manifest Destiny (see page 75). Lewis was rewarded with the first governorship in the territory. Clark arranged the publication of the duo's diaries and, when Missouri became a U.S. territory in 1812, served as its first governor. Sacajawea, whose name sparkles from numerous western monuments, is thought to have died among the Mandans around 1812, although a legend persists of her surviving in Wyoming to the age of one hundred.

T I D B I T S : ✪ *In the century following the acquisition, "Louisiana" provided land for fifteen states.* ✪ *Broken-down price for the Purchase: three cents an acre.* ✪ *Among the animals introduced to science by Lewis and Clark: the prairie dog, the jackrabbit, and the pronghorn.* ✪ *Other business, 1803: the Supreme Court decision in* Marbury v. Madison *establishes the principle of judicial review.*

"O Say Can You See by the Dawn's Early Light . . ."

Francis Scott Key, 1814

Americans indirectly owe their national anthem to a Maryland physician named William Beanes. In September 1814, as the British were preparing to bombard Fort McHenry, near Baltimore, Beanes was taken prisoner aboard a British ship for impeding His Majesty's troops' official looting. To the rescue came his friend Francis Scott Key, a Baltimore attorney. The release was negotiated on September 13, but both men were kept behind British lines until morning, as plans for the evening's attack had been discussed in their presence. It was at the end of that night's unsuccessful shelling, with "the rockets' red glare" and "bombs bursting in air," that Key wrote "The Star-Spangled Banner."

Benjamin Franklin had quipped after the Yorktown surrender that "the war of Independence was yet to be fought," and the conflict of which the Fort Henry episode was a part fulfilled that prophetic observation. By 1812, the United States was independent on paper, but her viability in the eyes of other nations—in terms of her ability to protect her citizens and her territory—was still in doubt. Specifically, her western lands were being harassed by border tribes in *ex officio* service to the British Crown, and her ships were being searched by British captains looking for contraband and "deserters."

England was still at war with Napoleon's France, and so it seemed fairly reasonable that she wanted to restrict enemy supplies. But the taking of American citizens was another matter. If one issue alone drove Americans to war with England for the second time in thirty years, it was the "impressment" of supposed British subjects into the ranks of George III's navy. Some of the American sailors thus impounded were, of course, British subjects, but many simply had the wrong accent.

Egged on by expansionist senators known as War Hawks, Congress declared war on Great Britain in June 1812. The subsequent two years were not exactly a string of successes for the new nation. On land, U.S. forces held Baltimore but lost Fort Dearborn (Chicago), Detroit, and Washington—which was burned by the British in 1814. The navy fared better, with successes on Lake Erie and in the Atlantic, where the forty-four-gun frigate *Constitution* earned its sobriquet "Old Ironsides." But overall the conflict moved toward stalemate rather than victory, and the Treaty of Ghent, signed in December 1814, put things back to the pre-war status quo. Ironically, the most famous American victory, Andrew Jackson's defense of New Orleans, came fifteen days *after* the ink was dry. Long-term memory being as short as it is, this eleventh-hour win convinced less reflective Americans that the United States had in fact won the war.

Key's masterpiece, set to the tune of an English drinking song, was printed as "The Defense of Fort McHenry" and immediately brought him local fame. As "The Star-Spangled Banner" it became nationally known, and it was picked up as a marching song during the Civil War. The U.S. Army made it an unofficial anthem during World War I, and the Congress made it official in 1931.

Performances of the national anthem before baseball games started in the rah-rah days of World War I and became a regular custom in World War II. By that time advances in public-address systems enabled singers, rather than bands, to belt out the song—which, as any listener will be quick to tell you, was a mixed blessing. Countless critics have suggested replacing the anthem with something less demanding, such as "My Country 'Tis of Thee" or "America the Beautiful"—but so far the traditionalists have won out.

"Our Country Right or Wrong"

Stephen Decatur, 1815

At the end of the eighteenth century, it was common practice for American merchant ships to pay tribute to the Moslem potentates of North Africa along the so-called Barbary Coast for protection from the rulers' own privateers. This cozy extortion scheme worked fine until 1801, when the pasha of Tripoli upped the ante, demanding an immediate payment of $225,000 for continued safety, at which time the Jefferson administration balked. In the resulting Tripolitan War (1801-1805), the actions of naval officer Stephen Decatur made him a national hero.

The son of a revolutionary war privateer, Decatur joined the navy in 1798, was sent to the Mediterranean three years later, and spent the entire war, as they say, "in theater." The most celebrated of his numerous colorful exploits was his 1804 scuttling of an American frigate, the *Philadelphia*, that had been captured by Tripolitan sailors. The episode earned him a captaincy—surely one of the few promotions in naval history given for the destruction of one's own vessel. Decatur went on to participate in the bombardment of Tripoli, overpower two enemy crews in hand-to-hand combat, and become the most dashing figure of the war.

He shone in the War of 1812 too, commanding the frigate *United States* in a celebrated victory over the British vessel *Macedonian* and managing to elude potential disgrace even after surrendering another vessel, the *President*, to a superior British force. In the public's eyes he could do no wrong, and the navy thought enough of his seamanship to send him back to the Barbary Coast in 1815, where he put an end to the piratical tribute system by forcing treaties on Tripoli, Tunis, and Algiers.

After his second return from the Mediterranean, Decatur was wined and dined nightly. At a Norfolk, Virginia, event, he offered this patriotic toast: "Our country! In her intercourse with foreign nations may she always be in the right. But our country, right or wrong." This last line has been a favorite with unreflective patriots ever since. Modern equivalents have included the Vietnam era's "America: love it or leave it" and the even less thoughtful "Support the president."

Always a scrapper, Decatur participated in at least three duels, the last of which did him in. His opponent was fellow officer James Barron, who in 1807 had surrendered his command, the *Chesapeake*, to a British ship seeking deserters. The incident fueled the anti-British feelings that led to the War of 1812, and Barron was suspended from duty. Decatur's resistance to his reinstatement led to the duel and his death in 1820. One newspaper responded, "Mourn, Columbia! For one of thy brightest stars has set."

TIDBITS: ✪ *G. K. Chesterton:* " *'My country right or wrong' . . . is like saying, 'My mother, drunk or sober.' "* ✪ *Speaking of duels—in the same year that Decatur sank the* Philadelphia, *the most famous duel in American history left Alexander Hamilton dead at the hands of Aaron Burr.*

Monroe Doctrine

James Monroe, 1823

In the second decade of the nineteenth century, several of Spain's possessions in Latin America revolted against the mother country and, following the lead of their northern neighbor, set themselves up as independent states. Reaction among European monarchs was not favorable, and around 1820 rumors began to fly that a Franco-Spanish alliance intended to reclaim the southern continent. At the same time, Russia was making noises in Alaska, thus imperiling the integrity of the Oregon Territory. To counter this dual threat to hemispheric peace, President Monroe in 1823 enunciated a "hands-off" policy known as the Monroe Doctrine.

Delivered in an address to Congress, the doctrine made four related points. One, the nations of the New World were "henceforth not to be considered as subjects for future colonization by European powers." Two, those nations were to be recognized as distinctively republican rather than monarchical. Three, any European moves into the Western Hemisphere would be taken as threats to the United States' peace and safety. Four, tit for tat: If the Europeans stayed out of "our" business, we would stay out of theirs. The total effect was to warn Europe away from a region the young country considered its backyard.

Americans responded enthusiastically, but the policy itself had little immediate effect. The monarchies kept their hands off less because of Monroe's posturing than because Great Britain, enjoying trade with the new Latin republics, implicitly stood behind the president's words. In 1845, however, President Polk reiterated the doctrine when he warned Britain out of disputed Oregon and away from the brewing Mexican War. Twenty years later, when French puppet Maximilian lost his Mexican throne after only three years in power, Monroe's principle of hemispheric hegemony seemed vindicated.

What gave Monroe's idea teeth was Teddy Roosevelt's celebrated "big stick" (see page 134). In the so-called Roosevelt Corollary, Roosevelt promised to exercise an "international police power" to restrain Latin American states guilty of "chronic wrongdoing." This policy, which added an American "hands on" intention to the original charter's "hands off" thesis, has led to the use of U.S. troops in the Dominican Republic, Cuba, Panama, Haiti, Nicaragua, and Grenada. So nettlesome had noninterventionist America's intervention become to Latins by the 1930s that TR's cousin, Franklin Delano Roosevelt, implemented what he called a Good Neighbor Policy, removing Marines from Haiti and releasing Cuba from a thirty-year vassalage under the Platt Amendment.

The long-term effects of the famous doctrine have been mixed. Hemispheric integrity has been preserved—if by that you mean that Europeans have left the Americas to their own headaches. But the security of New World "republicanism" is another matter, as is the attitude of Latin countries toward U.S. "protection." The U.S.-Cuba conflict since the 1950s, Puerto Rican separatism, disagreement within the Organization of American States—all point to the limitations of a principle that was at least as patronizing as it was well intentioned.

T I D B I T S : ✪ *Monroe originally wanted to issue a joint declaration with Great Britain. His secretary of state, John Quincy Adams, convinced him it would be unwise for the United States to seem "a cockboat in the wake of a British man-of-war." Adams's insistence that the United States act unilaterally makes him, as much as Monroe, the doctrine's author.* ✪ *The simmering slavery and tariff issues of the day were so masked by nationalist confidence in Monroe's administration that the time period is referred to as the Era of Good Feelings.*

"A Corrupt Bargain"

John Randolph, 1825

Monroe's Era of Good Feelings came to a crashing halt in 1824 after a notorious political tradeoff. The presidential candidates that year were war hero Andrew Jackson of Tennessee, the aloof Brahmin John Quincy Adams of Massachusetts, the capable but partially paralyzed William H. Crawford of Georgia, and Speaker of the House Henry Clay of Kentucky. The people's choice was clear: "Old Hickory" Jackson took more than 40 percent of the popular vote and 38 percent of the electoral. But 38 did not make up the required 51, and so the election was thrown into the House of Representatives, as stipulated by the Twelfth Amendment. Here "arrangements" ended up denying Jackson the presidency.

The Twelfth Amendment says that, in a case like this, the House members shall choose the next president from among no more than the top three runners. That left Clay out of the picture when it came to the running—but with a peculiar leverage when it came to the choosing. When Clay swung his votes to John Quincy Adams, the man from Massachusetts became president. The Jackson forces felt cheated—after all, the general had gotten fifteen more electoral votes than Adams—but they probably wouldn't have raised such a fuss if, several days after the decision, Adams hadn't made Clay his secretary of state. The sudden elevation of the Kentuckian to this post raised eyebrows and then angry voices.

One of the angriest was that of John Randolph, a Virginia congressman not especially known for his parlor manners. The apparent quid pro quo he called a "corrupt bargain." Clay himself he likened to a "rotten mackerel by moonlight," simultaneously shining and stinking. Finally Clay challenged Randolph to a duel, but as neither man could shoot off a pistol as well as his mouth, they both returned to the Congress unharmed.

This sad episode dogged Clay throughout a career that was in other respects extraordinarily distinguished. After entering Congress in 1806, he was perennially reelected—first as a representative, then as a senator—until his death in 1852. Known as the "Great Pacificator" for his deal-making acumen, he was, with Daniel Webster and John C. Calhoun, one of the "great triumvirate" of his period. His eloquence as one of the War Hawks helped us into the War of 1812, and his expertise at conciliation, forty years later, helped push through the Compromise of 1850. The presidency, however, continued to elude him. In addition to his somewhat opportunistic bow to Adams, he also lost to Jackson in 1832 and James Polk in 1844.

The bargain proved less than a bargain to Adams too. Painfully aware he was a minority president, he spent his time in the White House trying to push public works programs on a Congress and a populace that weren't interested. Three years after losing the 1828 race to Old Hickory, he returned to Washington as a Massachusetts congressman. His assessment of this reduced position was wryly humble. "No election or appointment conferred on me," he said, "ever gave me so much pleasure."

TIDBITS: ✪ *A nonconspiratorial reason for Clay's choice: Adams supported his "American System," which used high tariffs to protect U.S. manufacturers and encouraged a national network of roads and canals. Jackson didn't.* ✪ *Fervently suspicious of central government, Randolph once said that asking a state to limit its sovereignty was "like asking a lady to surrender a part of her chastity."* ✪ *Clay on his vain quest for the White House: "I would rather be right than be president."*

Tariff of Abominations

Protective tariff, 1828

In the nineteenth century, when the North was becoming heavily industrialized and the South was still largely agricultural, the protective tariff was a hot sectional issue. At no time did it generate more heat than in the election year of 1828, when supporters of Democratic candidate Andrew Jackson finagled to put together a tariff bill that would make the current president, John Quincy Adams, look ridiculous.

Adams, supported by Northern manufacturers, wanted a high tariff on foreign imports to protect the region's industry from competition. Jackson's Southern supporters resented having to subsidize Yankee factories and feared foreign retaliation against their own exported cotton, so they wanted the tariff kept low. To kill the bill, they adopted a strategy that backfired. They would support the high rates on foreign manufactures in exchange for equally onerous restrictions on wool and flax, which Northern factory owners needed for their mills. The idea was that the North *and* South would balk, and the Adams bill—along with his administration—would be defeated.

The Jacksonians won, but not the way they anticipated. The South stood fast against the bill, but not so the rest of the country. The flax- and wool-producing West welcomed protection for its raw materials, and the North proved willing to pay higher prices for those materials to maintain its virtual monopoly on finished goods. Result? The tariff squeaked by on eleven votes, with nobody really happy about it, and poor old John Quincy Adams got the blame.

But the defeat of a president was the least of the bill's repercussions. In the South, where it became known as the Tariff of Abominations, protest was fierce, with South Carolina flags being flown at half-staff and one observer recalling taxation without representation with the warning "Let the *New* England beware how she imitates the *Old.*" Newly elected Jackson's own vice-president, John C. Calhoun, was so outraged at the anti-Southern bill that he issued an anonymous document, the South Carolina Exposition, claiming that the states had a right to void a federal law within their borders if they thought it unconstitutional. This famous "nullification" doctrine—an extension of Jefferson's views on states' rights—was briefly adopted by South Carolina and remembered warmly by Southern secessionists in the coming decades. It also occasioned Massachusetts senator Daniel Webster's famous rejection of state autonomy: "Liberty and Union, now and forever, one and inseparable."

If Southerners thought that Old Hickory was going to pull their fat out of the fire, they were soon disappointed. He called nullification a "practical absurdity," equated disunion with treason, and snapped out, "Our Federal Union—it must be preserved." Calhoun came back with "the Union—next to our liberty most dear," but it was clear who was boss. In 1832 Calhoun resigned the vice-presidency to represent South Carolina in the Senate. There, as slavery's golden voice for two decades, he defended the institution so eloquently that even his antislavery foe John Quincy Adams credited him with "enlarged philosophic views" and "ardent patriotism." His dying words were "the South, the poor South."

TIDBITS: ✪ *Daniel Webster on the Tariff of Abominations: "Its enemies spiced it with whatever they thought would render it distasteful. Its friends took it, drugged as it was."* ✪ *Great Books of 1828: Noah Webster's* American Dictionary of the English Language; *Alexandre Dumas's* Three Musketeers.

"Old Hickory"

Jacksonian Democracy, 1829–41

The first six American presidents had been "old money" men. Southern planters or Boston Brahmins, they wore their leadership like a hereditary right and had no trouble fitting into John Adams's narrow view of government as the business of "the rich, the well born, and the able." Andrew Jackson was of a different breed. Yes, he had his share of aristocratic pretensions, but he also hailed from the "West," lacked a college education (a failing he shared with George Washington), and was unabashedly rough around the edges. His youth had been spent brawling and dueling, and he had acquired the name "Old Hickory" because of his legendary toughness on the battlefield.

His election in 1828 signaled the arrival of the so-called New Democracy. Up until about 1815, presidential nominees had been chosen by party caucuses and suffrage had been limited to the propertied few; it might be said, then, that presidents before Jackson were put in office by the majority of a minority. But by the 1820s, property qualifications were falling away—especially in such newly admitted Western states as Jackson's Tennessee—and a rising middle class was being heard. Wanting to appeal to this new electorate, Jacksonian politicians denounced the caucus system and promoted the novel idea that, in a democracy, everybody was fit to rule.

In his first address to Congress (given late in 1829), Jackson himself put it this way: "The duties of all public offices are, or at least admit of being made, so plain and simple that men of intelligence may readily qualify themselves for their performance. . . . In a country where offices are created solely for the benefit of the people no one man has any more intrinsic right to official station than another." The idea would have given John Adams chills, but it was definitely the wave of the future.

The broad-based appeal that Jackson embodied was his party's trump card, and today's Democrats trace their effectiveness to the "common man" pitch first sounded in Jackson's reign.

"Reign" is the right word, for this man of the people, wanting to represent their interests properly, brandished his presidential power so blatantly that his opponents called him "King Andrew I." From Washington all the way through to John Quincy Adams, the presidential veto had been employed a total of ten times; in his eight years as president, Old Hickory used it twelve. When South Carolina attempted to nullify the federal protective tariff, he got his troops ready and threatened the "nullies" with hanging. Most dramatically, he personally was responsible for the destruction of the national Bank of the United States, a "moneyed monster" based in Philadelphia.

Jackson's 1833 veto of the bank's recharter bill sent shudders through the "sound money" community, which felt that the state banks Jackson favored (his "pet banks," as they were known) were fiscally irresponsible and unreliable. But the common people loved it. To laborers, small businessmen, and farmers—all bridling under the bank's tight credit policies—getting rid of it was like sloughing off a millstone. Without the millstone, unfortunately, lending ran wild, ultimately resulting in the speculation-induced Panic of 1837—Jackson's legacy to his successor, Martin Van Buren. Van Buren's term, 1837–41, was the tail end of the so-called Age of Jackson.

The one segment of the "people" for whom the former general had little sympathy was the American Indian. He had made his reputation on the frontier as an Indian fighter, beating the Creeks at Horseshoe Bend in 1814 and burning Seminole villages in Spanish Florida a few years later. It was his administration that started the removal of the Five Civilized Tribes that culminated in the 1838 Trail of Tears (see page 69). Things would have been different, no doubt, had the Indians been permitted to vote.

"To the Victor Belong the Spoils."

William Marcy, 1831

Conventional wisdom has always blamed Andrew Jackson for bringing patronage—the notorious spoils system—into federal politics. But in fact, government appointments under Washington and Adams went exclusively to their Federalist supporters, and Jefferson, when he unseated Adams in 1800, followed suit by filling the posts with *his* cronies. The housecleaning that Jackson implemented in 1828 may have been no less partisan than that of his distinguished predecessors; certainly, it wasn't any more so.

Jackson's bad rap was the indirect result of a famous comment made by New York career politician William Marcy. The year was 1831, and Jackson had just appointed his closest adviser, former New York governor Martin Van Buren, ambassador to Great Britain. During the confirmation debate, Jackson's longtime foe Henry Clay attacked New York's party machine (known as the Albany Regency) and accused Van Buren of bringing patronage to Washington. Rather than denying the charge, Marcy jumped to his friend's defense by saying, in effect, "Sure—and why not?" Among his comments was this frank endorsement of his fellow New Yorkers:

They boldly preach what they practice. When they are contending for victory, they avow their intention of enjoying the fruits of it. If they are defeated, they expect to retire from office. If they are successful, they claim, as a matter of right, the advantages of success. They see nothing wrong in the rule that to the victor belong the spoils of the enemy.

From this speech came the unfortunate tag "spoils system"—as well as Old Hickory's guilt by association.

Marcy's crusty eloquence aside, Clay won the debate, the nomination did not go through, and Van Buren—who had counted his chickens too early—was forced to return from London the following spring. His opponents' cackles were short-lived, for in November 1832 he became vice-president; and four years later he followed Jackson into the White House. Marcy didn't do badly either. After his brief senatorial stint, he served three times as governor of New York, four years as secretary of war, and another four as secretary of state. The diplomatic plum of this last tenure was the Gadsden Purchase (see page 235, in the Appendices).

Political patronage continued to be the order of the day when it came to federal appointments until the 1883 Pendleton Act set up the federal Civil Service Commission and a system of competitive exams for government jobs. Its purview has since broadened considerably, so that today nine out of ten federal jobs are filled under Pendleton-type regulations. William Marcy would turn in his grave if he knew that letter carriers had to pass a written exam, although he no doubt would be pleased that the most prestigious nonelective offices at the federal level—judgeships and cabinet posts—may still be filled, quite legitimately, by party loyalists.

TIDBITS: ✪ *Most famous victim of the patronage system: President James A. Garfield, assassinated in 1881 by a party hack who didn't like the way he was distributing the spoils.* ✪ *Van*

"Remember the Alamo"

Texan Battle Cry, 1836

When Mexico won its independence from Spain in 1821, it welcomed Americans into its northern province of Texas, but these settlers soon became a liability. The three hundred families brought in by Virginian Stephen Austin in 1823 had swelled to thirty thousand strong within a decade, and few of them abided by the terms on which settlement had been encouraged. The immigrants, who considered themselves Americans, not Mexican citizens, resented the *federales* who had been sent to the province to keep order. They resisted conversion to Catholicism. And they brought slavery into the country, in direct violation of the Mexican constitution. When Antonio Lopez de Santa Anna set himself up as dictator in 1834, things were bound to come to a head, and they did so the following November, when American settlers set up a provisional government, ousted Mexican troops from San Antonio, and in effect claimed immunity from Mexican law.

Santa Anna reacted in 1836 by marching three thousand men toward San Antonio. Holed up there, in an abandoned mission called the Alamo, were about two hundred Americans, including the knife-wielding Jim Bowie from Louisiana, frontier congressman Davy Crockett from Tennessee, and the mission commander, attorney William Travis. Refusing offers to surrender, Travis determined to make a desperate stand, and did so, after repeated assaults, on March 6. When the Mexican army finally came over the walls, a handful of noncombatants were spared, but the armed defenders were all shot or bayoneted.

Almost immediately, "Remember the Alamo" became a battle cry, a reminder of the defenders' valor, and an encouragement to drive the Mexicans from "Texan" land. It was on everybody's lips a month later at San Jacinto, when Texans under the command of Sam Houston captured Santa Anna and effectively ended the war. Texas then became an independent nation—the Lone Star Republic—with Houston as its first president, and began agitating for admission to the Union. Since one of the causes for which it had fought, slavery, was becoming a hot political issue, admission was not automatic. Not until the accession of James Polk in 1845 was the infant nation absorbed by the United States.

On the eve of the final assault at the Alamo, Travis is said to have drawn a line in the sand with his sword, then asked the remaining defenders to choose death or flight by stepping over it if they wished to stay. Legend says all but one man crossed the line. This image, like that of the bedridden Bowie being carried over the line and of Crockett dying while swinging his rifle, "Old Betsy," as a club, has become a venerable motif in Texas folklore. Revisionist historians say that the line business may have happened, but there's no telling; and that Crockett was taken alive, tortured, and finally executed.

TIDBITS: ✪ *Spanish* Texas *comes from* tejas, *a Comanche word for "ally."* ✪ *Houston served two and a half terms as a Texas senator; he was forced out in 1861 when he refused to support secession from the Union.* ✪ *Texas's capital is named for Stephen Austin, its largest city for Sam Houston, and its second largest city for Polk's vice-president, George Mifflin Dallas.*

Trail of Tears

Cherokee Removal to Oklahoma, 1838–39

Most of the Indian tribes of North America adapted reluctantly and incompletely to white ways. Not so the Choctaw, Chickasaw, Cherokee, Creek, and Seminole, who lived in the Deep South. By the beginning of the nineteenth century, they had begun to wear European dress, convert to Christianity, build roads, run prosperous farms, and excel at trading. Thanks to the Cherokee leader Sequoyah, his tribe acquired a written language, which they used in 1827 to draft a constitution. Some Indians even went so far as to enslave imported Africans—at the time an ironic hallmark of an "advanced" civilization. True, renegade Creeks called Red Sticks fought the Americans bitterly during the War of 1812—providing Andrew Jackson with a military reputation—but for the most part the Southeast's red inhabitants earned their reputation as the Five Civilized Tribes.

Not that it did them any good. In 1790 a U.S. government treaty had granted the Creeks, for example, a rich expanse of land in highland Georgia; it pleased the government to have a buffer state near Spanish Florida. In 1817, however, when soldiers led by Old Hickory forced Spain to cede Florida to the United States, the Indians suddenly became expendable. In that same year the state of Mississippi was carved out of Choctaw and Chickasaw land, and two years after that Creek and Cherokee territory became Alabama. Almost immediately these two states, along with Georgia, began legislating their Indians out of existence—voiding tribal laws, invalidating their court claims, and encouraging the depredations of writ servers and liquor dealers. Within a decade the once-stable Indian communities had become victims of hunger, rum, and dispossession.

It fell to Jackson, elected president in 1828, to provide the finale to this sad mess. Petitioned by Indian leaders to support the 1790 agreement, he first balked, saying he didn't have the power, and then offered them replacement land out West. Acting under the Indian Removal Act of 1830, he in effect forced the tribes to exchange their verdant homeland for selected patches of the Great American Desert. When Jackson's own chief justice, John Marshall, decided in 1832 that Georgia's jurisdiction over the Indians was invalid, Old Hickory simply ignored the ruling.

"Removal," which took place throughout the 1830s, peaked in 1838 and 1839, as approximately fifteen thousand Cherokees were uprooted and force-marched toward the dusty plain then called Indian Territory. I say "toward" rather than "to" because one in four of the travelers never made it. Racked by cold, disease, and exhaustion, thousands died on the way, giving the exodus the doleful name "Trail of Tears." When the Indians arrived, they settled in under a new dispensation, which turned eventually into the same old charade. Promised Indian Territory for "as long as grass grows and water runs," they enjoyed their tenure for just fifty years. Pockmarked by squatters almost immediately, and slashed by a railroad in 1872, the territory was opened to "settlement" in 1889; less than twenty years later, it became Oklahoma.

TIDBITS: ✪ *For his role in subduing the Creeks, Jackson earned the nickname "Sharp Knife."* ✪ *A few hundred Cherokees escaped the Trail of Tears to hide out in the mountains of North*

Carolina; their descendants live there still, on a reservation.
✪ *Descendants of another group that refused the government's*
offer are the Seminoles of today's Florida Everglades.

The Peculiar Institution

Slavery in North America

In the last decades before the Civil War, Southerners called slavery their "peculiar institution," meaning that it was unique to the region. Its peculiarity in this respect was fairly recent, since the Northern states had only begun to abolish it in the 1770s, and as late as the 1840s pockets of slavery still existed in New Jersey. But if by "peculiar" you mean "weird," it certainly was that, and it had been so for more than two hundred years.

The weirdness started in 1619, when a Dutch ship brought the first Africans into Jamestown harbor. The institution spread gradually, chiefly in the South, where slaves provided cheap labor for plantation farming. In the eighteenth century they worked mostly on rice, sugarcane, and tobacco; it wasn't until the 1790s, when Eli Whitney's cotton gin facilitated the harvesting of that crop, that the stereotypically white-blanketed Old South became a reality. That invention rapidly changed the region's economy, and by the 1850s perhaps three-quarters of all field hands were exclusively or chiefly employed in growing cotton.

A dominant antebellum myth—one that remained popular as late as Margaret Mitchell's *Gone With the Wind*—depicts these unwilling workers as well fed, well clothed, and well treated.

That picture probably fit many plantations, for slave owners only occasionally were so stupid as to ruin their investments by starvation diets and abusive treatment. But the institution, in the best of cases, was hardly a clean one, and the image of the "happy darky" was tendentious fiction.

To begin with, slaves were snatched from their ancestral homelands, beaten into submission, branded, chained, and loaded onto ships that were little better than floating death camps. Those who survived the fetid crowding of the transatlantic "Middle Passage" were unloaded in the West Indies, separated from family members, sold at public auctions, and finally transported to their new "homes" in one of the Americas. If they ended up in the Old South, they worked there until they died, often with inadequate health care, no education (reading being prohibited), and little hope of ever enjoying the "blessings of liberty" that the Constitution promised to free men. Children could be sold off away from their parents, women could be "enjoyed" with impunity by their masters, and all slaves were subject to flogging.

That the slaves were not content with this setup is obvious from a variety of evidence. Black antebellum spirituals depict escape from worldly woes in images that are as obviously "anti-system" as they are religious. Thousands of slaves risked capture and punishment as "passengers" on the Underground Railroad. Countless more risked their lives in armed revolts. Most of these uprisings were small and quickly forgotten, but some were not. Gabriel Prosser in 1800, Denmark Vesey in 1822, and Nat Turner in 1831 all led large-scale slave rebellions that showed complacent whites the deepening cracks in the system's facade.

Nonslaves were also disturbed by the institution's peculiarity, and their attempts to abolish it were almost as old as the system itself. Pennsylvania Quakers took the lead, protesting slavery in the 1680s, but Southern whites were also divided early on. Thomas Jefferson tried (unsuccessfully) to get an antislavery clause into the Declaration of Independence in 1776. The nation banned slavery in the newly created Northwest Territory (today's Great Lakes states) in 1787 and outlawed the international slave trade—though not slavery itself—in 1808.

The official abolition of this Middle Passage, however, was little more than a flourish with a pen, because smugglers soon picked up the legal shippers' slack, and the system prospered, with all its flaws, for another half-century. From 1808 until 1865, when the Thirteenth Amendment freed all remaining slaves, the United States was in the decidedly peculiar position of debating the internal expansion of an institution whose importation it already had condemned. It took a civil war to resolve that contradiction.

T I D B I T S : ✪ *Although most slave owners had only a few slaves, the institution was numerically concentrated in the "planter aristocracy"; in 1860, more than half the South's slaves belonged to households owning twenty or more.* ✪ *First slave child born in North America: William Tucker (1624).* ✪ *Pseudoscience award of the century: to Louisiana doctor Samuel Cartwright, for dreaming up the "Negro" mental conditions* dyaesthesia aethiopica, *"leading to clumsiness," and* drapetomania, *"causing Negroes to run away."*

Underground Railroad

Antebellum fugitive slave network

The Underground Railroad was a clandestine, loosely organized network of escape routes that, in the three or four decades before the Civil War, helped thousands of Southern slaves flee north to freedom. To disguise their activities, railroad workers referred to the system's resting points—homes, barns, and other safe houses—as "stations" or "depots," to the slaves as "packages" or "goods," and to themselves as "agents" or "conductors." The system sent escapees as far north as Canada, although it was most active in Pennsylvania, Indiana, and Ohio: crossing the Ohio River served as a symbolic as well as actual passage into freedom.

The North Star Line (also known as the Liberty Line) operated largely under cover of darkness and in the face of the 1793 Fugitive Slave Law, which provided for the return to masters of escaped "property" and the fining or imprisonment of their abettors. In spite of these impediments, fugitives continued to flee on foot, in wagons, and by public conveyances. Neither a tougher Fugitive Slave Law (1850) nor the Dred Scott decision (1857) (see page 86), which reinforced slaveholders' claims, did much to stop this human flow. Generally accepted estimates place the number of successful escapes at one thousand a year, or perhaps fifty thousand in all.

Abolitionists, Quakers, and other liberal whites formed a staunch cadre of railroad operatives, often thwarting bounty hunters and masters' posses by concealing fugitive slaves in their houses. Valorous as this cadre was, however, the vast bulk of the railroad planning and administration was carried out by Northern blacks for their imprisoned kin.

The most famous of these freed-blacks-turned-emancipators was Harriet Tubman. Born into slavery around 1821, she escaped in 1849 and thereafter returned to the South nineteen times, leading an estimated three hundred slaves—including her own parents—out of bondage. Nicknamed "Moses," she was not someone you would like to cross: she was known to have persuaded reluctant "passengers" to come with her at the point of a gun.

According to legend, Tubman frequently announced departure times by singing the hymn "Steal Away" outside of slave cabins. True or not, that song did become an ineradicable part of American folklore. So did "Follow the Drinkin' Gourd," which enshrines the memory of one conductor, Pegleg Joe, who marked trails for fugitives in the direction of the Drinking Gourd—that is, the Big Dipper constellation, two of whose stars form a line that points to the nearby North Star.

TIDBITS: ✪ *With the outbreak of war, Tubman served the Union as a cook, nurse, and spy. Afterward, she ran an indigents' home in New York state, where she died in 1913.* ✪ *Most famous crossing of the Ohio River: Eliza, pursued by bloodhounds, in* Uncle Tom's Cabin.

"Manifest Destiny"

John O'Sullivan, 1845

When the Democrats nominated an obscure Tennessean, James K. Polk, for president in 1844, the Republicans jeered, "Who is James K. Polk?" Polk made them eat crow, as he not only beat the Whigs' Henry Clay, but became an extremely energetic chief executive. As the youngest person up to then elected to the presidency—he was forty-nine—Polk ran on an expansionist platform, promising a solution to the vexing Oregon question (see page 222) as well as the annexation of Texas, which had been trying for almost a decade to join the Union. His victory was widely perceived as a mandate for expansion, and Democratic journalist John O'Sullivan's call for the fulfillment of "manifest destiny" succinctly summed up Polk's foreign policy.

What O'Sullivan said, in the summer of 1845, was that America had a "manifest destiny to overspread the continent allotted by Providence for the free development of our yearly multiplying millions." He intended this *Lebensraum* philosophy to apply to Texas, but the phrase soon attached itself to the Oregon border dispute and, later in the century, to westward settlement in general: the Sioux, no less than Texas's Mexican landlords and Comanche nomads, were among the losers in the Democrats' grand design.

The most immediate effect of Polk's accession was the promised annexation of Texas (1845), pushed through Congress over antislavery objections. This led, within a matter of months, to war with Mexico, which felt its northern province had been wrested from it by Yankee fiat. After Mexican forces attacked a command under General Zachary Taylor near the Rio Grande in April 1846, Polk declared that the nation had been forced into war by the shedding of "American blood" on "American soil." Since the clash took place on disputed land, this characterization was pretty presumptuous, but Congress endorsed it, and war was declared on May 13. Two years later, by the Treaty of Guadalupe Hidalgo, the United States got not only Texas but (for a payment of $15 million) everything else from the Rio Grande to the Pacific—all of California, Utah, and Nevada and parts of Arizona, New Mexico, Colorado, and Wyoming. It was the biggest acquisition since the Louisiana Purchase.

Not everyone was fond of these developments. Illinois congressman Abraham Lincoln almost nipped his future in the bud by speaking out against Polk, and Henry David Thoreau, back in Massachusetts, protested the war by withholding his poll tax (he wrote *Civil Disobedience* to explain his position). But by and large the American people went along, happy to have added half a million square miles to their domain overnight at a cost of "only" thirteen thousand American lives.

One spinoff of the war was the Wilmot Proviso (1846), a congressional bill that sought to bar slavery from any territory that might be acquired as a result of the conflict. Although defeated, it surfaced the growing tension over an issue that would eventually divide the nation. The war also gave experience to young officers like U. S. Grant and Robert E. Lee. Both conceptually and tactically, then, the Mexican episode of manifest destiny was—in Thomas Bailey's words—"the blood-spattered schoolroom of the Civil War."

TIDBITS: ✪ *A Mexican Alamo: the castle of Chapultepec in Mexico City, where one hundred teenage cadets—Los Niños to the Mexican people—fell before U.S. forces.* ✪ *In jail for tax evasion, Thoreau supposedly was asked by Ralph Waldo Emerson, "What are you doing in there, Henry?" His reply: "What are you doing out there?"*

Forty-Niners

Nineteenth-century gold rushes

Although an itch for good farmland was probably the primary impulse behind westward expansion, gold fever ran a solid second. In the second half of the nineteenth century, hundreds of thousands of would-be strike-it-richers left their homes in the East for far-flung gold fields, and at least three states— California, Colorado, and Alaska—were settled originally by these hopeful prospectors.

Of the great American gold rushes, the first and most famous was California's. It started in 1848, which, propitiously, was the same year that the territory went from Mexican to U.S. control. That January, carpenter James W. Marshall spotted gold. He was partner to Swiss adventurer John A. Sutter, who owned a sawmill near Sacramento. The pair's attempts to keep the find secret until they could lock in their claim ran aground on the rumor express, and by the following year eighty thousand fellow adventurers had poured in. These "Forty-Niners," as they became known, transformed a sparsely populated region into a patchwork of boomtowns and seething commerce. San Francisco alone jumped from eight hundred to thirty thousand souls, and in 1850 this fortune-hunters' paradise became a state.

Eight years later, in Colorado, the pattern repeated itself. Gold was found at Cherry Creek, near today's Denver, and within months perhaps 100,000 hopefuls had set their sights on this new El Dorado. Many painted "Pikes Peak or Bust" on their wagons, unaware until they neared their objective that the gold fields were sixty miles from that landmark. Those who returned disillusioned replaced their original signs with "Busted, by God," although enough stalwarts settled in the Rockies to make Colorado a U.S. territory in 1861.

The third major find, in Canada's Klondike region, brought thousands to these Yukon wastes in 1897–98, and many of them spilled over into Alaska, where a lesser-known but profitable rush also developed. The Yukon discovery played itself out within a few years, but not before providing plenty of material for writer Jack London and poet Robert W. Service.

Miners' dreams also played a part in the growth of Nevada's Virginia City and in opening up South Dakota's Black Hills to white settlement. The Black Hills gold find led eventually to the last great Plains Indian war—but it was not only there that gold and red mixed poorly. In the ten years after the Sutter's Mill find, for example, at least half of California's estimated 100,000 native people were killed in what one historian has called "the biggest single spree of massacring in American history." The colorful prospector, in other words, served as point man for Indian extermination.

"Go West, Young Man."

John Lane Soule, 1851

Legend has the crusading newspaperman Horace Greeley (1811–72) speaking this line to a young man who has asked his advice for prospering in life. The actual originator was Greeley's fellow editor John Lane Soule, who published it in the *Terre Haute Express* in 1851. But by using it in dozens of *New York Tribune* editorials, Greeley made it into a household phrase. So in terms of popular usage Greeley certainly "owned" the sentiment.

"Uncle Horace" was how his readership knew him, and if the moniker conjures up images of a slightly dotty character, that is perfectly in line with Greeley in the flesh. Had anybody thought to hold a contest around 1850 for America's greatest living oddball, it would have been a photo finish between Thoreau and Uncle Horace. (My money would have been on Uncle Horace.) Thoreau dabbled in utopian thinking from time to time; Greeley devoted a lifetime to it, championing such causes as abolitionism, free land for homesteaders, free schools, temperance, black suffrage, and amnesty for former Confederates. Most of these eventually took root nationwide—proving, perhaps, the cynic's observation that outrageousness plus twenty years equals common sense.

Like Thoreau, Greeley was also physically outrageous. Balding, bespectacled, and sporting chin whiskers that looked like they had been thrown on him with a pitchfork, he favored a flop hat, white slicker, and grubby farmers' boots. Yet when he wrote, the nation listened; in barroom and kitchen, from New York to the trans-Mississippi West, Greeley wielded an influence on American political thought that was not equaled until the days of William Randolph Hearst's yellow journalism. For thirty years the American common man saw Uncle Horace as a kind of populist Solomon. In a common joke of the 1850s, a small-towner is asked what he thinks of a certain political question. "Dunno yet," he says. "I never read the *Tribune* till after dinner."

One of Uncle Horace's heroes was French writer Charles Fourier, whose dream of a socialist utopia inspired numerous communes, notably Brook Farm, where, in the 1840s, Charles Dana and Nathaniel Hawthorne unsuccessfully sought salvation in dirty fingernails. Greeley's championing of such agrarian experiments was perfectly consistent with his advocacy of westward expansion and his push in particular for passage of the Homestead Act. "Vote Yourself a Farm," Greeley and other back-to-the-landers urged the electorate, and the opening of the West that followed that 1862 act owed much to their exhortations.

A New Hampshire–born abolitionist, Greeley helped to found the Republican party, backed Lincoln in spite of his more cautious approach to slavery, denounced the graft-ridden Grant administration, ran against the General himself in 1872, and was defeated thanks to the skewerings of cartoonist Thomas Nast, who depicted him as a publicity-hungry crank. He died less than a month after the election.

"Bleeding Kansas"

1850s Catchphrase

In the first half of the nineteenth century, congressional compromises postponed three times the "irrepressible conflict" that New York senator William Henry Seward predicted slavery would precipitate. In the first trade-off—the 1820 Missouri Compromise—Congress dealt with the nettlesome issue of allowing slavery in the Louisiana Territory. North of 36° 30′, the southern boundary of Missouri, the territory was declared free, but Missouri itself came in as a slave state, and—to mollify Northern sentiment—Maine entered as a "balancing" free state. The second compromise—the Compromise of 1850—was drawn to fix the status of lands acquired in the Mexican War. It admitted California as a free state, paid slaveholding Texas ten million dollars to release its claims on lands disputed with New Mexico, opened up the entire Southwest between Texas and California to "popular sovereignty" (whereby the residents themselves would vote on slave-or-free), abolished the slave trade in the District of Columbia, and strengthened the toothless Fugitive Slave Law. The debate on this compromise has been called the greatest in the nation's history; its stars included the "immortal trio" of Henry Clay, John C. Calhoun, and Daniel Webster—and sparky newcomers Stephen A. Douglas and William Seward.

Four years later, Douglas was largely responsible for the third and most momentous postponement, the 1854 Kansas-Nebraska Act. The catalyst for this act was a transcontinental railroad, which everybody wanted built, but on whose eastern terminus nobody could agree. For years Southerners fought against Chicago because a line from there would pass through Nebraska Territory—guaranteed free soil by the Missouri Compromise. Douglas, who as an Illinois senator *and* a railroad stockholder may have been a tad biased toward the Windy City, won the opposition over by pushing popular sovereignty: We'll build the road through the Nebraska Territory rather than Texas, he said, but we'll let the settlers there decide for themselves whether they want to have slavery. And we'll also divide the Territory into two states, Nebraska and Kansas, so that each can choose abolition or slavery for itself. The idea was that Nebraska would opt for abolition while Kansas, next to slave-state Missouri, would choose slavery.

Douglas's deal, which the South accepted, instantly repealed the free-soil promise of the Missouri Compromise, led to the founding of the Republican party to fight further expansion of slavery, and turned Kansas, overnight, into a killing field. Seeing that numbers would now decide the issue, both slavers and abolitionists sent "settlers" into Kansas. Highlights of the ensuing Border War between Kansas and Nebraska included the May 1856 sacking of the town of Lawrence by a posse of proslavery "Border Ruffians"; and the immediate retaliation by abolitionist John Brown, who killed five slavers in the so-called Pottawatomie Massacre. Throughout the fifties, the place was known as "Bleeding Kansas."

Kansans continued to fight, but with ballots as well as bullets. Ballot-stuffing helped proslavery forces pack the territorial legislature and even submit a proslavery constitution for congressional approval in 1857. To his credit Douglas, smelling fish, got it sent back to the plains for a referendum, where it was defeated in a free-soil landslide. Bleeding Kansas then quieted down until 1861, when as the thirty-fourth state it defended the Union in the war its own troubles had foreshadowed.

TIDBITS: ✪ *Within two years of their famous compromise, all three of the "immortal trio" were dead.* ✪ *When New York clergyman Henry Ward Beecher supported the shipment of rifles to Kansas free-soilers, the weapons became known as "Beecher's Bibles."*

Uncle Tom's Cabin

Harriet Beecher Stowe, 1852

Upon meeting Harriet Beecher Stowe in 1862, Abraham Lincoln is reputed to have said, "So you're the little woman who wrote the book that made this great war." Hyperbole, but not by much. The New Englander's antislavery novel sensitized hundreds of thousands of people to the abuses of the peculiar institution, and if she can't be said to have actually started the conflagration, she certainly threw on her share of tinder. Not even Tom Paine's *Common Sense* had had a greater impact on the thinking of Americans about the need for a war.

Born in Connecticut in 1811, Harriet Beecher moved to Cincinnati in 1832, where her father, the celebrated preacher Lyman Beecher, had accepted the presidency of a theological seminary. She stayed in Ohio for almost twenty years, marrying Bible scholar Calvin Ellis Stowe, bearing seven children, and observing at close hand the institution of slavery, which flourished across the Ohio River in Kentucky. She came from good abolitionist stock—her father and two brothers were active free-soilers—but maternal responsibilities prevented her, until 1850, from joining them in the antislavery crusade.

In that year two things happened that turned the professor's wife into the country's most talked-about novelist. First, the Stowes moved to Brunswick, Maine, where Calvin was to teach at Bowdoin College. Second, as part of the Compromise of 1850, Congress passed a Fugitive Slave Act that provided harsh penalties for harboring escaped "property." With more money and leisure than she had known in years, Harriet reacted to Congress's move by writing *Uncle Tom's Cabin*. Originally published serially in the abolitionist paper *National Era*, it became a book in 1852. Within a year it had sold 300,000 copies—and by the end of the decade, perhaps a million. Widely translated abroad, it also reached millions of people in staged versions.

The book, which was subtitled "Life Among the Lowly," depicted the trials of the piously sentimental Uncle Tom, the young mulatto mother, Eliza, and her child, Harry, as they confront the evils of a system floridly symbolized by the Northern-born overseer Simon Legree. It has been derided frequently as melodramatic, but it's surely no more deserving of that charge than other nineteenth-century popular novels, and in any event the point was propaganda, not Flaubertian realism. Stowe's sister-in-law Isabel, in urging her to write, had suggested something "that would make this whole nation feel what an accursed thing slavery is." Harriet responded with flying colors. Her success was such that in the 1850s "Uncle Tomitude" became a chiding synonym for sympathy with blacks.

A second antislavery novel, *Dred: A Tale of the Great Dismal Swamp*, failed to achieve an equal popularity, and so Stowe turned to quiet, charming portraits of her native New England until her death in 1896.

"A House Divided Against Itself Cannot Stand."

Abraham Lincoln, 1858

Lincoln was never as militantly against slavery as the radical abolitionists, but he was far less accommodating than his senatorial opponent, Stephen A. Douglas. His famous "house divided" speech indicates why. In 1858, after the newly formed Republican party had asked the then Illinois lawyer to be its candidate for the Senate against the Democrats' Douglas, Lincoln lost no time in attacking the "Little Giant" for his mediatory "popular sovereignty" doctrine, which allowed each territory individually to decide whether to permit slavery within its borders. At the nominating convention, Lincoln scorned Douglas for dodging the moral issue and suggested that a "let the people decide" posture would, sooner or later, expand slavery. The most memorable nugget of his speech went like this:

> A house divided against itself cannot stand. I believe this government cannot endure, permanently half slave and half free. I do not expect the Union to be dissolved—I do not

expect the House to fall—but I do expect it will cease to be divided. It will become all one thing, or all the other.

This "all one thing, or all the other" idea didn't sit well with Republicans, who feared it would be read as extremist. They had cause to worry, because that's exactly how the Democratic candidate depicted it. In the famous Lincoln-Douglas debates of that summer, the Little Giant sang states' rights all the way, hinting not only that Lincoln was abolitionist, but that he was advocating a "war of sections."

The debates were complicated by a recent Supreme Court ruling that had every tavern in the country buzzing with the words "Dred Scott." Scott was a Missouri slave who, having accompanied his master to free Illinois and to Wisconsin Territory (free of slavery according to the Missouri Compromise), claimed to have been automatically freed by his presence there. A Missouri court bought this, but his plea was lost on appeal, and in the 1857 Supreme Court decision, Chief Justice Roger B. Taney pulled the rug out. His majority decision, citing the Fifth Amendment, said that no slaveholder could be deprived of his property without "due process" and that Scott, as a result, was still a slave. Taney's message, like Douglas's in the Kansas-Nebraska Act, was that the Missouri Compromise was null and void.

Abolitionist Horace Greeley called the Dred Scott decision "the closing in of an Arctic night in our history." Lincoln's party called it a "wicked and false judgment," and Lincoln himself, seeing that the ruling could be construed to refer to Illinois as well as to Wisconsin, feared the Court might next rule that the Constitution "does not permit a *state* to exclude slavery from its limits. . . . We shall lie down pleasantly dreaming that the people of Missouri are on the verge of making their State free, and we shall awake to the reality that the Supreme Court has made Illinois a slave State."

Lincoln also saw that Dred Scott was in conflict with Douglas's own pet idea, popular sovereignty. At a debate in Freeport, Illinois, he asked the Little Giant to explain how the people of a territory could exclude slavery if slaves like Scott were simultaneously permitted there. Douglas's response, as subtle as it was pragmatic, was that "slavery cannot exist a day or an hour anywhere unless it is supported by local police regulations." True in the abstract, but small comfort to Mr. Scott. This so-called Freeport Doctrine alienated Douglas from hardcore slavers, but it won him the Illinois election, and Lincoln had to wait two years to return to Washington.

TIDBITS: ✪ *The "house divided" line is from Mark's Gospel, where Jesus, accused of using the devil to cast out devils, responds, in effect, "That's illogical." Lincoln's point exactly.* ✪ *Lincoln's assessment of Douglas's moral position on slavery: "He don't care about it."* ✪ *Dred Scott was freed by his owner shortly after the decision but died a year later in St. Louis.*

"I Wish I Was in the Land of Cotton."

Daniel D. Emmett, 1859

Ironically, the two American songsmiths most closely associated with the South were Yankees. Stephen Foster was born in Pennsylvania and died, drunk and broke, in New York. Dan Emmett, author of "Dixie," was born and died in Ohio. The son of a blacksmith, Emmett learned music from his mother and quickly became a versatile performer. At seventeen he joined a military band as a fifer; three years later he was a drummer for a circus; in his twenties he sang and played banjo with "Daddy" Rice, star of an early minstrel troupe; and in 1843, playing fiddle, he led his own Virginia Minstrels to quick success. The troupe's blackface performances of stereotypically "Ethiopian" song and dance made them a favorite with Northern audiences and helped to establish, if not invent, minstrel conventions.

After a brief tour of England, Emmett returned in 1857 to New York, where he joined the Dan Bryant Minstrels. He had been writing songs for that troupe for two years when Bryant, one Saturday, suggested he write a snappy tune for Monday's show. Emmett holed up with his fiddle, and when he emerged, he had composed a bouncy "walk-around" for the troupe's plantation number based on a Southern catchphrase, "I wish I was in Dixie Land." He called the song "Dixie Land," but everybody else called it "Dixie."

It took the country by storm. New Yorkers whistled it in the streets. President Lincoln loved it. So did Jefferson Davis, who had it played at his inauguration as Confederate president. In the South it brought lumps to so many throats that the boys in gray soon made it their marching song, and it has been the region's unofficial anthem ever since. Emmett himself was a little shaken by this appropriation, because it made him suspect of harboring Confederate sympathies, and in 1863 he penned some pro-Union lyrics that nobody now remembers.

The lyrics that everybody remembers begin by recalling what made the Old South what it was. "The land of cotton" was no descriptive flourish. The entire regional economy rested on King Cotton, and it is not going too far to suggest that the ultimate cause of the Civil War was "cottonocracy." In the couple of decades before the war, half of all U.S. trade revenues came from the South's cotton exports; by 1860, the cotton take was almost 60 percent. Since the profitability of this major resource depended entirely on unpaid black labor, the cotton lords saw opposition to slavery as more than a philosophical opinion; to them, it was economic terrorism. The War Between the States, as they call it in the South, was fought *in* the land of cotton and *over* it.

As for "Dixie," popular opinion has it that this common term for the South reflects the Mason and Dixon line established in 1769 as the border between Pennsylvania and Maryland. Some scholars say that a New Orleans bank issued ten-spots in the 1850s bearing the French term *dix* (for "ten") on the reverse, and that the "Land of Dixies" was thus originally Louisiana. A minority opinion speaks of a kindly slave owner named Dixie who lived in the eighteenth century on Manhattan Island; when his slaves were sold down South, they sang longingly of "Dixie's Land" as a lost Eden. (No Southerner in his right mind accepts this interpretation.)

T I D B I T S : ✪ *Emmett's middle name, Decatur, recalls the adulation of naval officer Stephen Decatur around 1815.* ✪ *The best-known blackface troupe (for whom Foster wrote) was the Christy Minstrels. They should not be confused with the 1960s folk group the New Christy Minstrels.* ✪ *"Uncle Dan" Emmett's other hits: "Old Dan Tucker" and "Blue Tail Fly."*

"John Brown's Body Lies Amouldering in the Grave."

Civil War song, ca. 1860

As a group, the abolitionists were odd ducks. Seeing slavery as a moral abomination, they fought the system with every means at their command, breaking whatever laws were necessary to make themselves heard, imperiling their reputations—

and sometimes their lives—in support of their views. Moderates like Abraham Lincoln and Stephen A. Douglas might debate compensating owners for emancipation or extending slavery into the western territories. But to those who saw slavery as "a covenant with death and an agreement with hell," such quibbles were worse than irrelevant; they nourished the beast.

Individually, abolitionists were as eccentric as they were zealous. The movement's unofficial high priest, William Lloyd Garrison, founded the American Anti-Slavery Society in Philadelphia in 1833 and denounced the system in his weekly *Liberator* for thirty years. In addition to renouncing his American citizenship, he proposed that the free North secede from the South and, in response to the Kansas-Nebraska Act, publicly burned a copy of the Constitution. Garrison's right-hand man, Boston Brahmin Wendell Phillips, actually announced a curse on that hated document for permitting slavery and banned slave-grown sugar and cotton from his home. Lucretia Mott reacted to the 1850 Fugitive Slave Act by opening her Pennsylvania home to runaway blacks. Henry Ward Beecher, to dramatize the evils of bondage, turned his Brooklyn church into a mock slave market. Frederick Douglass, himself a former slave, formed Negro regiments during the Civil War and, at the age of sixty-seven, took a white wife.

And then there was Ohio farmer John Brown. The son of an early abolitionist, Brown moved his family to a black community in 1849, formed a League of Gileadites to help runaways, served as an agent on the Underground Railroad, and brooded increasingly on plans to free the slaves by force. The 1854 Kansas-Nebraska Act sent him, withering with conviction, to Bleeding Kansas, where, with four of his sons, he spread the free-soil message by killing a group of proslavery settlers. The attack, which took place in Pottawatomie, was quickly dubbed the Pottawatomie Massacre.

After two more years of Kansas raiding, Brown moved in

1859 to a Maryland farm. Using it as a base of operations, he planned an attack on the U.S. arsenal at Harper's Ferry, Virginia, which he hoped would yield the guns and ammunition needed to supply a guerrilla army of freed slaves. Poor planning scotched the attempt. Brown lost two sons in a firefight with U.S. Marines; badly wounded himself, he was arrested on October 17 and tried for treason. Since insanity ran in his family, Brown certainly could have mounted a non compos mentis defense; he chose not to. Instead, he treated the court to this farewell:

> I believe that to have interfered in behalf of His despised poor I did no wrong, but right. Now if it is deemed necessary that I should forfeit my life for the furtherance of the ends of justice, and mingle my blood further with the blood of my children and the blood of the millions in this slave country, I say let it be done.

Without much delay it was done. Brown, calm and unrepentant, was hanged on December 2 and was transported at once to abolitionist martyrdom.

The earliest sign of his martyrdom was the appearance of the memorial song "John Brown's Body," set by some anonymous bard to an old religious melody. Within a year Union troops were marching to the words "John Brown's body lies amouldering in the grave/But his soul is marching on." Within two years, they had changed the words but not the tune, after Boston poet Julia Ward Howe turned out "The Battle Hymn of the Republic." Its fulsome but catchy opening went like this:

> Mine eyes have seen the glory of the coming of the Lord
> He is trampling out the vintage where the grapes of wrath are
> stored
> He hath loos'd the fateful lightning of His terrible swift
> sword
> His truth is marching on

Union troops quickly made this more literary lyric as popular as the dirge for Brown, and the two have enjoyed equal fame for more than a century.

Howe was a piece of work in her own right. In addition to writing other, more forgettable lyrics, she was an ardent abolitionist and—like many of that breed—a fighter for international peace and women's suffrage. She was also a popular lecturer on social reform, a speaker of four languages, and the first biographer of the feminist Margaret Fuller.

TIDBITS: ✪ *The commander of the Marines who took Brown into custody at Harper's Ferry was a Virginia gentleman named Robert E. Lee.* ✪ *The tune common to "John Brown's Body" and the "Battle Hymn" came from "Say, Brothers, Will You Meet Me," written by minister William Steffe.* ✪ *Most famous appropriation of Howe's lyrics: John Steinbeck's depression-era novel* The Grapes of Wrath.

Emancipation Proclamation

Abraham Lincoln, 1863

The mythic Lincoln—somber, upright, and ever vigilant for Liberty—freed the slaves in 1863 because he could not tolerate the continued oppression of God's creatures. The actual Lincoln freed them—or, rather, made a gesture in the direction of their liberation—out of a combination of ethics and expediency.

Lincoln was clearly repelled by slavery. As early as 1831 he had announced, "If I ever get a chance to hit that thing, I'll hit it hard!" After the 1846 Wilmot Proviso suggested banning slavery from any territories to be acquired from Mexico, Lincoln voted for it more than forty times. His opposition to the peculiar institution was also clear in his 1858 debates with Stephen Douglas. To the abolitionists, though, he was too moderate. They did not appreciate his famous observation to Horace Greeley, made in 1862: "If I could save the Union without freeing any slave, I would do it; and if I could save it by freeing all the slaves, I would do it; and if I could save it by freeing some and leaving the others alone, I would do that."

When he signed the freedom order one month after that remark, it was from a blend of righteousness and reality. He favored extending freedom, certainly, but he also intended the move to isolate the South internationally, by making it more difficult for her European sympathizers to continue their support. Because Lincoln had seemed to be waiting for a Union victory before acting, Richard Hofstadter slights the proclamation as having "all the moral grandeur of a bill of lading." Historian Claude Nolen's view is more generous:

> Lincoln moved toward abolition when he believed he could do so effectively. Early in the war, steps toward emancipation would have lost the border slave states to the Confederacy, and so lost the war. Moreover, Northern public opinion would have rejected emancipation as a war aim until the casualties of prolonged conflict made freedom for blacks, and corresponding enlistment of black troops, acceptable goals. Lincoln encouraged and waited on this change in public opinion.

On September 17, Union forces won a long-awaited victory at Antietam. Five days later the president announced a "preliminary" proclamation—in effect, a warning to the Southern states that, if they didn't surrender by January 1, their slaves would be free on that day. When the New Year came without a Confederate response, Lincoln issued the official Proclamation.

The actual effect of the famous document has been much debated. It did sever the South from Europe, and so had the desired international result. But domestically its immediate effect was not apparent. Certainly it didn't free a single slave. Since it referred only to slaves in *rebellious* states, masters in the loyal border states—Maryland to Missouri—were permitted to keep their slaves without prejudice. In the Confederacy, on the other hand, the order was moot, because U.S. authority over the region had not been decided. Historian Thomas Bailey has observed nicely that, when Lincoln set out to free the slaves, "where he *could* he would not, and where he *would* he could not." A London paper reacted to the Proclamation's wording even more caustically: "The principle is not that a human being cannot justly own another, but that he cannot own him unless he is loyal to the United States." American slaves were not in fact emancipated until the ratification of the Thirteenth Amendment in 1865. The Great Emancipator, who pushed for it strongly, had then been dead for eight months.

TIDBITS: ✪ *Reactions to the Proclamation ranged from Horace Greeley's "God bless Abraham Lincoln" to the Dixie epithet "Lincoln the fiend."* ✪ *The Chicago Historical Society held the original draft of the Proclamation until 1871, when it was destroyed in the Great Chicago Fire.*

"Four Score and Seven Years Ago"
Abraham Lincoln, 1863

We owe the most famous speech in American history to a combination of shallow graves and threats of rain. In the summer of 1863, Gen. Robert E. Lee, heading seventy thousand men, had mounted the South's last great offensive against the North. He got as far as Gettysburg, Pennsylvania, before his soldiers battled an even larger force of Union troops in what proved to be the turning point of the war. By July 4, Lee was retreating toward Virginia, and the Pennsylvania fields were littered with fallen bodies—at least seven thousand on the Union side alone. Buried hastily where they fell, they were bound to be unearthed by autumn rains unless a more permanent and suitable place for graves could be found. To that end Pennsylvania purchased land for a Soldier's National Cemetery. Lincoln dedicated that resting place on November 19.

The words he spoke over the dead that day might never have been delivered at all had not the affair's organizer, David Wills, asked the president—almost as an afterthought—to share the honors with the principal speaker, Edward Everett. A former congressman, governor of Massachusetts, and president of Harvard, Everett was the nation's foremost orator, and at Gettysburg he proved true to form, spinning out periodic sentences and classical allusions for two hours in a spirited condemnation of rebellion. What Lincoln added to Everett's learned harangue was two minutes of softly mumbled but deathless prose. It's short enough—and good enough—to quote in full:

Four score and seven years ago, our fathers brought forth on this continent a new nation, conceived in liberty and dedicated to the proposition that all men are created equal. Now we are engaged in a great civil war, testing whether that nation, or any nation so conceived and so dedicated, can long endure. We are met on a great battlefield of that war. We have come to dedicate a portion of that field as a final resting place for those who here gave their lives that that nation might live. It is altogether fitting and proper that we should do this. But in a larger sense, we cannot dedicate, we cannot consecrate, we cannot hallow, this ground. The brave men, living and dead, who struggled here, have consecrated it far above our poor power to add or detract. The world will little note nor long remember what we say here, but it can never forget what they did here. It is for us the living, rather, to be dedicated here to the unfinished work which they who fought here have thus far so nobly advanced. It is rather for us to be here dedicated to the great task remaining before us, that from these honored dead we take increased devotion to that cause for which they gave the last full measure of devotion—that we here highly resolve that these dead shall not have died in vain—that this nation, under God, shall have a new birth of freedom, and that government of the people, by the people, and for the people shall not perish from the earth.

Although half the throng could not hear the president, and the rest were just starting to listen when he reached the end, literary opinion was nearly unanimous in admiration. *Harper's* magazine called the speech as "simple and felicitous and earnest a word as was ever spoken." The *Springfield Republican* called it a "gem." Edward Everett graciously wrote Lincoln the next day, saying, "I should be glad, if I could flatter myself that I came as near the central idea of the occasion, in two hours, as you did in two minutes."

The central idea, as Lincoln presented it, was that the North was fighting to preserve the Founding Fathers' ideals of equality, liberty, and popular rule. To Lincoln those dreams were embodied in the Union cause, and indeed in the idea of "Union" itself. Although his dedication to equality—for blacks and women, for example—was no more progressive than that of his generation, he was thoroughly committed to the preservation of the national experiment that, in his wonderfully archaic phrasing, went back "four score and seven years" to 1776. Coming less than a year after the Emancipation Proclamation, the Gettysburg Address may reasonably be seen as underscoring the slaves' "new birth of freedom," which was consistent with the preservation of a "new nation" wed to the "proposition that all men are created equal."

TIDBITS: ✪ *Contrary to legend, Lincoln did not write the speech in the train on the way to Gettysburg, or on the back of an envelope. The surviving first draft is written on White House stationery.* ✪ *Numerous speakers had used the "of, by, for" bit before; Lincoln picked it up from an antislavery pamphlet by Theodore Parker.*

"War Is Hell."

William Tecumseh Sherman, 1879

A fuller version of Sherman's famous comment—delivered to the graduating class of a Michigan military school on June 19, 1879—went like this: "I am sick and tired of war. Its glory is all moonshine. It is only those who have never fired a shot nor heard the shrieks and groans of the wounded who cry aloud for blood, more vengeance, more desolation. Some say that war is all glory, but I tell you, boys, it is all hell."

Sherman was certainly in a position to know. As commander of the Union's western theater in 1864, he visited more hell on the South than anyone else had done in four years. In May he began an invasion of Georgia that would cripple the Confederates' supply capacity and, in the process, make "Sherman" the ugliest sound in eleven states. Throughout the summer, Sherman fought his way toward Atlanta—a fearsome process brilliantly evoked in *Gone With the Wind*—and in September he put the city to the torch. In November he led his sixty thousand hated "Blue Bellies" on a sixty-mile-wide march to the sea, destroying everything of military value on the way between smoldering Atlanta and the port city of Savannah. He then turned north, wreaking equal destruction throughout the Carolinas until stopped by the Confederate surrender the following April.

The most famous "scorched earth" campaign in American history, Sherman's march left central Georgia—the "garden spot of the Confederacy"—a wasteland of charred plantations, twisted rail lines, and trampled crops. It was the first incidence of all-out war on American soil, and it earned the general the unenviable nickname of "Sherman the Brute." Quite possibly it shortened the war by its debilitating thoroughness, but saying that to a Southerner is like painting Truman as a life-saver to the Japanese.

After the South's surrender, Sherman was sent West, where he protected transcontinental railroad workers from Indian attacks. In 1869 his former superior officer, President Grant, made him commanding general of the army, and he served in that post for fourteen years. When he retired, the Republicans attempted to draft him for president, but he put them off with another memorable line: "If nominated I will not run. If elected I will not serve." Like Calvin Coolidge years later, he kept his word.

TIDBITS: ✪ *Sherman's middle name was after the Shawnee chief Tecumseh, a powerful force for Indian resistance until his death at the Battle of the Thames in 1813.* ✪ *The general's younger brother John, sponsor of the Sherman Anti-Trust Act, wasn't a bit shy about seeking the presidency: he tried three times without success.*

"Now He Belongs to the Ages."

Edwin M. Stanton, 1865

On April 9, 1865, three days shy of four years after the South's 1861 attack on Fort Sumter that started the Civil War, the conflict effectively ended. In the Virginia town of Appomattox Court House Robert E. Lee surrendered his disheveled troops—known as "Lee's Ragamuffins"—to Ulysses S. Grant. The jubilant Union soldiers had to curtail their celebration because Grant felt it inappropriate on such a solemn occasion. Five days later the Union at large suffered a similar muting of its joy, when an actor sympathetic to the South, John Wilkes Booth, shot President Lincoln in Washington's Ford's Theater. When Lincoln died the next morning in a house across the street, his war secretary, Edwin M. Stanton, pronounced this brief, touching eulogy at his bedside.

Ironically, Stanton had long opposed Lincoln's policies. He had fought Lincoln's nomination in 1860 because he felt—correctly, as it turned out—that his election would precipitate secession. At one point he referred to his future chief as "the original gorilla," and although he served ably in the war post, he also contributed to the internal dissension that made the Lincoln cabinet one of the testiest on record. Staying on after the assassination, he also proved an irritant to Lincoln's successor, former vice-president Andrew Johnson. Feeling that the South deserved a punitive peace, Stanton joined the Radical Republicans in staying the administration's soft hand, and he was largely responsible for Johnson's impeachment.

His comment on the slain leader's historical importance was prophetic, since Lincoln, almost immediately after his death, acquired a halo that he had never worn in life. Thousands of people turned out to watch the railroad car that brought his body back to Illinois for burial. Booth, who died days after the shooting in a fight with Union soldiers, joined Benedict Arnold and Aaron Burr as a modern Judas. "The ages" soon painted the fallen president not as a human being with political faults and personal failings, but—in the words of more than one posthumous accolade—as "the American Christ." Selective memory later did the same thing for John F. Kennedy.

As was true after the Kennedy assassination, conspiracy theories soon bred like flies. In Lincoln's case, at least, there was proof that the crazed Booth had not acted alone. On the same night that Lincoln was shot, the secretary of state, William Seward, was also attacked. Rumors abounded that a cabal of revolutionists was out to bring down the government by "propaganda of the deed," and four suspects were arrested, tried, and hanged. Among them was Mary Surratt, the first woman executed for treason in the nation's history.

T I D B I T S : ✪ *The play that Lincoln and his wife were watching when he was shot was the comedy* **Our American Cousin.** ✪ *John Wilkes Booth's brother Edwin was the most famous Shakespearean actor of his day; his portrayal of Hamlet is ranked up there with Laurence Olivier's.*

Carpetbaggers and Scalawags

Radical Reconstruction, 1867-77

With the end of the Civil War, the nation faced mammoth readjustment problems. As at the end of all wars, there were ravaged populations, scarred land, devastated production facilities, and bills to pay: the national debt was $3 billion, which, for 1865, was an incredible sum. But there were also problems stemming from the peculiar nature of the conflict. Millions of former slaves were now free. How were they to fit into postwar society? The rebellious states were now ready—if not entirely willing—to be brought back into the Union. How was that to be managed? On what grounds would readmission take place? Would the South have to pay reparations? And what of the rebellion's leaders? They had been responsible for the deaths of hundreds of thousands of young Yankees; should they be punished, pardoned, or what?

While the war was still going on, Abraham Lincoln had given conciliatory answers to these questions. "With malice toward none, with charity toward all" was how he had put it in his second inaugural address. "To bind up the nation's wounds," the president had said, the wayward states should be welcomed back without prejudice: as long as 10 percent of a state's voters were willing to swear allegiance to the United States, they could form a new government, free of slavery, and be recognized.

This sounded good to the South, but hard-liners in the president's party made it impossible to achieve once the war was over. Led by Charles Sumner of Massachusetts and Thaddeus Stevens of Pennsylvania, the so-called Radical Republicans rejected Lincoln's plan and a similar plan submitted by his successor, Andrew Johnson. Vowing to punish the South for treason, they blocked the seating of Southern Democrats in the Congress and, in 1866, passed the first Reconstruction amendment to the Constitution. To counter the oppressive "black codes" that Southern states were passing to regulate free blacks, this amendment—the Fourteenth—gave ex-slaves citizenship and all the civil rights that went along with it. It also "encouraged" the former rebels to give blacks the vote by reducing states' representation if they refused to do so, barred former Confederates from public office, and repudiated the South's enormous debt.

Since Southerners didn't exactly rush to take this medicine, the Radical Republican Congress force-fed it to them, via the Military Reconstruction Act of 1867. This act divided the South into five military districts, each one run by a district commander in Union blue with the authority to oversee elections and appoint officials. For the next ten years, martial rule ran the South, making Reconstruction extremely unpopular in old Dixie. Former slavemasters didn't take to their former "property" standing alongside them at the polls, illiterate whites resented illiterate blacks having equal electoral privileges, and everybody hated being bossed about by Yankee soldiers.

The greatest animosity, however, was reserved for the functionaries who helped the soldiers run the system. Southern collaborators with the Blue Bellies were known as "scalawags." Yankee financiers who streamed in to bolster (or milk) the system were called "carpetbaggers" after the peculiar luggage they brought with them. Many of these supposed puppets of Uncle Sam worked ably to reconstruct the broken South, and the integrated legislatures of the period were no slouches either: they set up poor relief, funded construction, and established schools. But the bad eggs—and there were many—discredited the system by making governance merely an excuse for pocket lining. One enterprising carpetbagger administrator managed to save $100,000 in a year—on an $8,000 salary.

Reconstruction engendered a bitterness that is still felt in the South today, but it also had more immediate ramifications. For one thing, white supremacists used it as an excuse to form such groups as the Ku Klux Klan. For another, it caused the impeachment of Andrew Johnson, on the trumped-up charge that he had illegally fired an appointee; in reality, Radical Republicans were irritated at his soft line toward the South. (They missed kicking him out of office by only one vote.) And it led to the Hayes-Tilden "deal" of 1876.

With the vote count from four states in dispute, the presidential election of that year was effectively deadlocked. A special commission was set up to decide the tally. Although Democrat

Samuel Tilden had a clear majority of the popular vote, the nod went to Republican Rutherford B. Hayes—along with a notorious quid pro quo. In exchange for following Grant into the White House, Hayes agreed to remove the last federal troops from Southern territory, thus effectively ending Reconstruction. Without military support, black gains were soon undone by rampant Klanism. Exit carpetbaggers, enter Jim Crow (see page 111).

TIDBITS: ✪ *Tennesseean Johnson, a former tailor, hated the planter aristocracy and so remained personally loyal to the Union even after secession. During the war he had represented the pro-Union, eastern portion of the divided state in Congress.* ✪ *Thaddeus Stevens's commitment to equality did not end with his death: he was buried, at his request, in a black cemetery.* ✪ *The second Reconstruction amendment, the Fifteenth, established black voting rights in 1870.*

The Gilded Age
Mark Twain and Charles Dudley Warner, 1873

The quarter-century after the Civil War might be called the wild oats period of American history, so rife was it with bumptious energy, slack morals, and ingenious cupidity. Most of the country's great industrial fortunes were either made or consolidated in this period. Indeed, in President Grant's administration (1868–76), go-getters and palm-greasers were so clearly in the saddle that the nation's leader might have been nicknamed "U. S. Graft."

So many people were on the take that one historian has

referred to the era as the Great Barbecue, "with the state supplying the beef." Historically, the period is better known as the Gilded Age. The tag came from a novel by Mark Twain and Charles Warner that ridiculed the hollowness beneath the veneer of material progress. Although space does not permit a full accounting of the "creative financing" scams that oozed through the former general's regime, here are three of the most famous:

✪ *Black Friday.* In the summer of 1869, financiers Jim Fisk and Jay Gould began buying all the gold they could get their hands on, while spreading rumors that a price rise was unstoppable, since Grant had agreed not to sell federal reserves. In fact Grant had made no such agreement, but credulous speculators climbed on the bandwagon, hiking the price up even further. When the government then released its reserves on "Black Friday" (September 24), the smaller players were ruined. Of course, Fisk and Gould had already sold, at a tidy profit.

✪ *Credit Mobilier.* In a story that broke in 1872, officials of the government-supported Union Pacific Railroad were discovered to have created a shadow firm, the Credit Mobilier, to build their transcontinental phenomenon, then submitted inflated construction bills to the railroad and pocketed the difference. Among the national figures who had accepted Credit Mobilier shares (seemingly as a bribe to keep mum) was Grant's vice-president, Schuyler Colfax.

✪ *Whiskey Ring.* This one, which came to light in 1875, was a conspiracy among whiskey distillers and government officials to divert liquor taxes into the Republican party's treasury. When Grant first heard about it he waxed indignant, crying, "Let no guilty man escape." When his personal secretary, Orville Babcock, was implicated, he backed off, and the culprits were acquitted.

There were other scams, less well known, and there were private pirates as well, unconnected to Pennsylvania Avenue. The most notorious of these was New York's "Boss" William

Tweed, head of the city's Democratic machine (Tammany Hall), who bilked the taxpayers of at least $50 million before being jailed for fraud in 1873. Grant can hardly be blamed for the depredations of the opposing party, but it was his watch, and he did set the tone. As many historians have pointed out, he was a bad judge of character rather than venal himself—but that was quite enough to keep the beef sizzling.

T I D B I T S : ✪ *Jay Gould, whose financial wizardry ruined many, once called himself, with perverse pride, "the most hated man in America."* ✪ *Tweed was brought down—at least in part—by the unflattering cartoons of Thomas Nast, whose pen gave us the Republican elephant, the Democratic donkey, and the American Santa.* ✪ *Answer to Groucho Marx's most famous question ("Who is buried in Grant's Tomb?"): the president and his wife, Julia.*

"Mr. Watson, Come Here, I Want You."

Alexander Graham Bell, 1876

On March 10 of the country's centennial year, the Scottish-born inventor Alexander Graham Bell spilled acid on himself in his Boston laboratory. Reflexively calling for help, he summoned his assistant, Thomas Watson. Nothing momentous there, except that Watson was in another room. The message, delivered over "telephonic" wires, got Watson to do his boss's bidding—and became the first words ever transmitted by Bell's invention.

Bell had a long-standing, practical interest in the transmission of speech. Like his father and grandfather before him, his professional work was in the teaching of the deaf, first in Scotland, then England, Canada, and finally Boston, where in the 1870s he taught vocal physiology at Boston University. In 1876, at the age of twenty-nine, he had been working for several years to perfect a technology that would carry vocal-cord vibrations over wire. The March 10 victory was a culmination of those efforts.

Bell introduced his device to the public at Philadelphia's Centennial Exposition, where it won a gold medal and brought him instant fame. The next year he founded the company that bore his name. Patent law being what it was in the 1870s—decidedly unreliable, that is—Bell fought for years to secure the monetary reward that clearly was his due. His chief rival was the Western Union Telegraph Company, which in 1876 hired Thomas Edison to invent a mechanism that would compete with Bell's device while enabling them to avoid paying him royalties. Three years of litigation ended in an agreement that Western Union would stay out of the telephone business if the new Bell Company would steer clear of telegraphy.

A Renaissance man to rival his rival Edison, Bell tinkered with, among other things, air conditioning, sheep breeding, metal detection, jet propulsion, and human flight. Devices he invented anticipated both the helicopter and the hang glider, while his metal detector was used in 1881 to search for the lodged bullet that eventually did in President Garfield. He was also a founding member of the National Geographic Society and the father-in-law of its longtime president, Gilbert Hovey Grosvenor.

TIDBITS: ✪ *Bell's father, Alexander Melville Bell, invented "visible speech," which showed deaf people the position of the vocal organs during talking.* ✪ *Until its dismantling by the government in 1984, the successor to Bell's company, AT&T, owned twenty-two regional phone networks.* ✪ *The unit of volume, decibel, is taken from Bell's name.*

Custer's Last Stand
June 25, 1876

The most famous battle of the Plains Indian wars had the same cause as the others: a white government promised Indians land, then found a better use for it and rescinded the promise. In this case the promised land was the Black Hills of South Dakota, sacred to the Sioux; the better use was the mining of gold, discovered there in 1875. The rescission came late that year when the army gave tacit approval to intruding prospectors by refusing to block their access or ferret them out. The Plains tribes had been losing ground for a decade to just such incursions, and they finally determined to protect their sacred space at all costs. That winter, under the leadership of the medicine chief Sitting Bull and the warrior Crazy Horse, they began to leave the reservations and gather in Montana. George Armstrong Custer's mission was part of a master plan to bring them to heel.

Custer commanded the U.S. Seventh Cavalry, and his unit's part in the master plan was clearly defined. He was to follow the renegades' trail up the Rosebud River, moving slowly so that another force, under the command of General John Gibbon, would have time to position itself to the hostiles' north. Then the two columns would converge on the Sioux, attacking them in a classic pincers movement.

But Custer was not used to moving slowly—or, for that matter, to following orders. In the Civil War he had acquired a reputation as a lucky daredevil, courageous under fire to the point of recklessness, and this had made him, briefly, the youngest general in U.S. Army history—quite a feat for someone who had finished last in his class at West Point. People spoke, some with admiration and some with bitterness, of "Custer's Luck," and that luck served him well in almost ten years on the Plains. He survived a one-year suspension for the mistreatment of prisoners, dissension from his officers for failing to rescue one of their number from a fatal ambush, and even a second suspension at the hands of President Grant, one of whose relatives he had implicated in shady dealings. But on June 25, at the Little Bighorn River, his luck ran out.

Custer's doom was the result of his own poor judgment. First, he split his command into four columns, each designated to scour a different patch of hostile ground. As any ROTC student can tell you, this kind of thing is ill advised when you don't know the enemy's numbers. Second, he ignored his superiors' orders to take it slowly. He wanted to make sure Gibbon wasn't going to have all the glory. Third, he ignored the reports of his own scouts that the Little Bighorn was teeming with far more warriors than even the Seventh Cavalry could handle alone. While some say he was betrayed during the fight by disloyal officers who refused to come to his aid when they heard firing, few historians will dispute the fact that his judgment was lacking.

Nobody knows exactly what happened in the fight itself, but the outcome of the encounter is not in doubt. By nightfall of June 25, the entire command—more than two hundred men—lay dead on a ridge above the Little Bighorn, their bodies naked and mutilated, their scalps hanging in Sioux and Cheyenne lodges. The news reached the East Coast newspapers just before the July 4 weekend of the nation's centennial year. It didn't make for extra Roman candles.

Almost overnight the "boy general" was transformed into an American Roland as the Custer myth took off at a gallop. Poems, plays, novels, and biographies transformed "Autie" into a national martyr, and within months every beer-chugger in the country knew exactly how he had died, from the Anheuser-Busch painting. That the activity in that famous tableau was totally invented did nothing to undermine Yellowhair's growing legend.

For the Indians, Custer's Last Stand soon proved a disaster deferred, since the federal government, shocked and embarrassed, made the extermination of remaining hostiles a national priority. Crazy Horse was killed at an Indian agency a year after his greatest victory. Sitting Bull fled to Canada, remained there for several years, and surrendered to U.S. forces in 1881. Nine years later, the Plains wars ended at Wounded Knee, South Dakota, when hundreds of Sioux fell to the bullets of Seventh Cavalry soldiers who had been children when the sainted Custer died.

TIDBITS: ✪ *A tireless self-promoter, Custer wrote* My Life on the Plains *in 1874; his wife, Libby, followed up with a trio of volumes that ensured his posthumous reputation as the hero of his age.* ✪ *The fair-haired boy was a lieutenant colonel in 1876, his Civil War generalcy having been a wartime-only promotion. And his hair was short during his Last Stand; he'd had it cut before the battle.* ✪ *Most romanticized movie biography: Raoul Walsh's* They Died with Their Boots On, *with Autie Custer played by Errol Flynn.*

Jim Crow Laws

Segregationist legislation, 1870s–1960s

In an attempt to protect newly enfranchised blacks from discrimination, the Reconstructionist Congress passed not only the Fourteenth and Fifteenth Amendments—stipulating, respectively, "equal protection" under the law and voting rights—but also two Civil Rights Acts, which guaranteed equal access to public accommodations. Within months after President Hayes kept his back-room promise and removed federal troops from the South, this legal bulwark began to fall apart, as lawmakers at both the state and local levels passed statutes institutionalizing segregation. This new legislation—the so-called Jim Crow laws—stayed on the books for eighty years.

Jim Crow was a stage persona of the antebellum minstrel star Thomas Rice, with whom Dan Emmett, among many others, served an apprenticeship. The application to segregationist laws was appropriate, for their purpose was to position blacks as "happy darkies," stuck forever in the legal impotence of the prewar years. Ironically, the separation that they enshrined was less a feature of the Old South than of the new. Before the war, blacks and whites had had frequent contact—as a large mulatto population made clear. Only later, when former slaves had become voters, did race-mixing begin to be perceived as a social horror.

Segregation was never exclusively a Southern phenomenon. The Northern states had their own versions of Jim Crow, and the federal government too got into the act. In 1883, the Supreme Court struck down an 1875 civil-rights act as unconstitutional. Thirteen years later, in *Plessy v. Ferguson*, it upheld a Louisiana law requiring "separate but equal" accommodations on public railways. The majority opinion in this famous case held that the Fourteenth Amendment did not mandate social equality, but only the literal "equal protection of the laws." Dissenting justice John Harlan wrote that "our Constitution is color blind, and neither knows nor tolerates classes among citizens." He wrote eloquently, but he spoke alone.

With eight of nine justices giving the nod, racist legislatures had a field day. Blacks soon had not only their own "equal" lunch counters and hotel rooms and grammar schools, but their own bus seats and park benches and water fountains. Virtually every facet of Southern life was affected by this divide-and-conquer stratagem, and those who questioned it risked night riders' beatings, torture, and lynchings.

Such Klan "justice" was far from uncommon. To protect the legal fiction of "separate but equal," white supremacists with fearsome regularity accused their black neighbors of crimes against the system—rape, murder, or "disrespect" would all do—and executed them, often by hanging, without trial. Between 1880 and the 1940s, it has been estimated, more than four thousand blacks met their fates in this manner. Not until 1954, in *Brown v. Board of Education*, did the Supreme Court overturn the *Plessy* decision.

TIDBITS: ✪ *Before the Civil War, Kentucky-born Harlan was proslavery. When critics mocked his switch to a civil-rights posture, he responded, "Let it be said that I am right rather than consistent."* ✪ *First prize for nose-thumbing Jim Crow goes to Jack Johnson, the black heavyweight boxing champion (1908–15) who for seven years defeated "white hope" challengers while touring the country with a white wife.*

"The Public Be Damned."

William H. Vanderbilt, 1883

The expansion of the U.S. rail network after the Civil War is one of the great business stories of all time. In 1865 there were about 35,000 miles of track in the country, most of it in the Northeast. By the end of the century, the rails had spanned the continent *four* times and covered 200,000 miles. This vast network not only facilitated the settlement of the West, but also provided jobs for thousands of workers (especially the Irish and the Chinese); opened eastern markets for the West's produce; stimulated related industries such as oil and steel; and—not least of all—made fortunes. By 1900, railroad families like the Stanfords, the Harrimans, and the Vanderbilts had created a nouveau-riche American aristocracy.

The game had its losers, though. The Plains Indians lost a way of life when the Iron Horse chugged and spat through the prairies, scattering buffalo and spawning instant towns. Investors lost their bankrolls in stock-watering schemes that managed to raise construction money through the sale of worthless shares. And to the many small shippers who used the lines to make a living, it seemed that the great public also lost. It was not so much that the railroads' managers profited from kickbacks and bribery, but that, in setting their rates, they revered no god other than maximum profit. This attitude—the dominant business attitude of the day—benefited stockholders at the expense of minor customers, who could be wiped out by fickle or onerous charges.

Few businessmen in the late 1800s, of course, thought there was anything else to business *but* making money. In an age when Adam Smith's laissez-faire gospel and William Graham Sumner's social Darwinism undergirded most capitalist thinking, profit maximization was a sacred cow. Oddball entrepreneurs like Rochester's George Eastman or New Jersey's Robert Wood Johnson might concern themselves with the needs of such "stakeholders" as customers, employees, and the general public, but for most capitalists, private enterprise was just that.

When railroad king William Vanderbilt was asked, therefore, whether he didn't run his lines "for the public benefit," his famous response was in keeping with the times: "I don't take any stock in this working for anybody's good but our own. . . . We like to do everything possible for the benefit of humanity in general, but when we do, we first see that we are benefiting ourselves. Railroads are not run on sentiment, but on business principles, and to pay."

The damned public, of course, didn't take kindly to such frankness. Like critics of corporate greed today, many saw Vanderbilt's admission as an arrogant boast rather than a statement of principle. There was considerable resentment of the railroad millionaires and of other "robber barons." By the 1880s, with the nation increasingly split into haves and have-nots, that resentment flared into a demand for government control over the most visible, and most arrogant, of the industrial giants. Accordingly, in 1887, Congress established an Interstate Commerce Commission to regulate the railroad barons' perceived abuses, particularly the use of rebates and discriminatory charging.

It took a while for the ICC to develop a bite—its early rulings were constantly overturned by the Supreme Court—but it set a precedent for the government oversight of Big Business that grew into the Washington bureaucracy we know today. Business leaders who condemn this morass as a drag on free enterprise forget that government control was the desperate reaction of a scorned populace to cavalier indifference. Had the robber barons been less contemptuous of the public, their descendants might now be regulating themselves.

TIDBITS: ✪ *Completion of the first transcontinental railroad: the "Golden Spike" ceremony linking the Union Pacific and the*

Central Pacific lines at Promontory Point, Utah, on May 10, 1869. First crack at the spike was by Central Pacific president Leland Stanford. ✪ *Stanford funded California's Stanford University; the Vanderbilts gave us Vanderbilt University, in Tennessee.*

"Give Me Your Tired, Your Poor . . ."

Emma Lazarus, 1883

On the pedestal of the Statue of Liberty, a bronze plaque carries the words of Emma Lazarus that, for a century, have spelled "welcome" to a nation of immigrants. The New Yorker's poem "The New Colossus" was written in 1883 and is a typical sonnet with fourteen lines of iambic pentameter. Most often quoted are these final five:

> Give me your tired, your poor,
> Your huddled masses yearning to breathe free,
> The wretched refuse of your teeming shore.
> Send these, the homeless, tempest-tost to me.
> I lift my lamp beside the golden door!

Moving stuff, but before you get too choked up, it's best to recall that not all Americans were as welcoming as Lazarus or Lady Liberty. True, America had been a haven for Europe's "huddled masses" for centuries; true, too, that economic opportunity—the "golden door"—had been a lodestar for most of them. But the openness of which Lazarus boasted had vied, throughout U.S. history, with the xenophobia of already-established immigrants, and specifically with Anglo-Saxon "nativist" elements that saw the open door as letting in mongrel hordes.

In the 1850s such purist thinkers formed the American (or "Know-Nothing") party, which ran Millard Fillmore for president in 1856 on a platform that shrieked, "Keep the Catholics out!" As immigration swelled after the Civil War—and particularly as the "refuse" of *southern* Europe began to arrive in what is known as the New Immigration—nativism enjoyed a rebirth, with the new targets of fear the "swarthy" races: Latins, Slavs, Jews, and (most of all) Orientals. The first restrictive immigration laws, passed one year before Lazarus wrote her poem, banned paupers, convicts, criminals—and Chinese.

The New Immigrants continued to flood in, at a clip of about half a million a year, until the Johnson-Reed Act of 1924. This established a limit of 150,000 new arrivals a year from outside of the Western Hemisphere and split that total up into national quotas. Since the quotas were based proportionally on population percentages as of 1890, the law ensured Western Europe's demographic dominance and prevented an influx from Asian and African nations; in fact, Johnson-Reed banned the Japanese altogether. The McCarren-Walter Act of 1952, although it did admit Asians, did little to offset the European bias, and it has been only in the last twenty-five years that quotas have effectively acknowledged the Third World.

Many would argue that xenophobia is as alive today as it has ever been. Press reports of Japan-bashing and, more recently, Arab-baiting, do not dispel that impression, as the United States, like its rival the former Soviet Union, continues to wrestle with the dilemmas of multi-ethnicity. Writing in 1782, the Frenchman Michel-Guillaume-Jean de Crèvecoeur said that in America "individuals of all nations are melted into a new race of men." Picking up the metaphor in 1908, the British Jewish writer Israel Zangwill defined a governing American myth, praising intermarriage in his play *The Melting Pot*. Given the dogged immiscibility of many groups, though, this assimilationist metaphor is now being reexamined. With "cultural pluralism" currently the fashionable ideal, some historians have suggested it might be more accurate to replace the melting-pot metaphor with the "salad bowl."

TIDBITS: ✪ *Official name of the Statue of Liberty: "Liberty Enlightening the World." ✪ Main contributors to the Old Immigration: England, Germany, Ireland—and, if you count the unwilling, Africa. ✪ Main contributors to the New Immigration: Italy, Austria-Hungary, Russia.*

Haymarket Riot
May 4, 1886

The year 1886 marked a turning point for the American labor movement. In that year, a London-born cigar maker named Samuel Gompers founded a trade-union confederation that would dominate labor activism for more than a generation, while in Chicago less conciliatory labor activists were wiped out virtually overnight when they were implicated in an "anarchist attack" on the city's policemen.

In the early 1880s the country's dominant labor organization was Terence Powderly's powerful Knights of Labor, an agglomeration of perhaps 700,000 working people whose goal was the formation of a single, national union. The Knights' distinguishing characteristic was its inclusiveness—unskilled as well as skilled workers, blacks as well as whites, women and men alike—and by mid-decade this inclusionist policy had borne fruit. Under the banner "An injury to one is the concern of all," the Knights waged several successful strikes and were rapidly gaining support for their principal goal: the establishment of an eight-hour day.

Unfortunately, they were joined in their struggle by a host of more radical allies, whose association in the public mind with the Knights eventually dealt labor a fierce blow. There were, for example, the members of Daniel DeLeon's Socialist Labor party, who advocated public ownership of the "means of production"—meaning Mr. Carnegie's and Mr. Rockefeller's industries. There were other socialists, less well organized, who resided in every city that boasted an immigrant population. Last but not least, there were the anarchists, the leftmost fringe of a disaffected labor population, who favored more the elimination of private property than its redistribution. The least temperate of these radicals, New York's Johann Most, distributed leaflets with assembly instructions for homemade bombs.

New York and Chicago both had strong anarchist factions, but the movement's center was the Windy City, with editor August Spies's *Arbeiter-Zeitung* (Worker's Times) serving as the sounding board for a largely German activism. On May 3, 1886, police clashed with a group of strikers, killing one and wounding several others. Spies called for a massive protest in the city's designated soapbox arena, Haymarket Square. Turnout was tepid, but the speeches were hot, and when the police started to disperse the crowd, somebody rolled a bomb in their direction. Seven were killed, and the remaining cops' return fire left four workers dead.

For American anarchism, the results of the Haymarket "riot" were disastrous. Although evidence of his involvement was slim, Spies—along with seven of his friends—was convicted of murder. Of the group, Spies and three others were hanged, one killed himself in his cell, and the other three—six years later— were pardoned by liberal governor Peter Altgeld, whose career was instantly ended by this act of clemency. For the Knights, the outcome was no more salubrious. Although they had had no involvement whatsoever in the incident, as labor's point men they too took a fall: the eight-hour-day movement lost steam, and by 1890 membership in the Knights had dwindled to 100,000.

The vacuum was quickly filled by Samuel Gompers. His American Federation of Labor, unlike the Knights, concentrated on organizing *skilled* workers, which gave it a greater immunity from strike-breaking than the Knights had ever enjoyed. Gompers was also less political than his predecessors, preferring to concentrate on bread-and-butter issues rather than systemic change. Socialist unionists in the 1880s had denounced "wage slavery" as one insidious part of a corrupt whole; Gompers proclaimed, "The way out of wage slavery is higher wages." With this willingness to work for change *within* the system, the AFL acquired the Knights' fallen mantle.

Not that this instantly solved labor's problems. Conditions continued to be objectionable enough to generate two massive strikes in the 1890s—the Homestead Strike of 1893 and the Pullman Strike of the following year—and it wasn't until the Clayton Anti-Trust Act of 1914, which exempted unions from the Sherman Act's "trust" definition, that federal favor started to swing in the direction of labor. It has swung back and forth ever since.

TIDBITS: ✪ *The skilled-worker bias of the AFL led to a famous break in 1935, when a splinter group favoring industry-wide membership formed the Congress of Industrial Organizations. The two reunited twenty years later as the AFL-CIO.* ✪ *Socialist Eugene Debs, leader of the Pullman Strike, ran five times unsuccessfully for president.* ✪ *The System's concession to an increasingly militant working population: the establishment of Labor Day in 1894.*

How the Other Half Lives

Jacob Riis, 1890

Virginia farm boy Thomas Jefferson had warned at the turn of the nineteenth century that urbanism, that European vice, could ruin the country. History ignored him, and by the end of the century, with thousands of Americans leaving farms and seeking their fortunes in the cities, our metropolises had become lodestones for precisely the troubles that agrarians feared: drunkenness, disease, vagrancy, violence, and greed. New York, swollen by immigrants as well as disenchanted farmers, was the worst of the lot. In 1890, about half of the city's 2.7 million inhabitants were sardined into generally dilapidated, often lightless, and always filthy cold-water walk-ups. Here, beset by sweatshop owners on the one hand and indifferent landlords on the other, they scrabbled to make a living in the promised land while their children shared the streets with typhus and whores.

Jacob Riis, a Danish carpenter, arrived in this brick-and-mortar dystopia in 1870. After surviving for years on the edge of starvation, he became a police reporter, with his principal beat being the immigrant-rich Lower East Side, an area he called the "foul core" of the city's slums. Here he wandered, usually at night, for more than a decade, writing stories for the *Tribune* and the *Sun*, photographing the tenements' wretchedness, and taking notes for a phenomenal exposé. *How the Other Half Lives*, published in 1890, brought the reality of slum life home to thousands who had never seen the inner city. The book so effectively rubbed the nation's nose in its own sewage that slum clearance became a reformist priority, and legislators started writing building codes.

To Riis, the heart of the slum problem was private greed. Landlords expected their properties to bring in 30 or 40 percent in profit return—a rate they could get only by neglecting their buildings. The universal tenant complaints were "that they were entirely uncared for, and that the only answer to their requests to have the place put in order by repairs and necessary improvements was that they must pay their rent or leave." Similar complaints are still made today, and with good cause, but today's slum dwellers have options that Riis's neighbors could not have imagined: rent control, tenant councils, and civil suits. Such protections are due in no small part to Jacob Riis.

Like many first-generation immigrants, Riis was a fanatic assimilationist. He proudly entitled his autobiography *The Making of an American,* and a subtext of his famous exposé was that learning English was a prerequisite to gaining improved conditions. Melting-pot prejudice also shows in his ethnic stereotyping—the "sensual" Negro, the "thrifty" German, and so on—but such bias was not peculiar at the time, and it certainly didn't mute his concern for his impoverished subjects. What he said of the slum's children was also implicit in his understanding of their elders: that they are "naturally neither vicious nor hardened, simply weak and undeveloped, except by the bad influences of the street."

The success of *How the Other Half Lives* brought Riis to the attention of Theodore Roosevelt, who was New York's police commissioner in the 1890s. Occasionally Roosevelt accompanied the reporter on his nocturnal rounds, and out of this association grew a lifetime friendship. The Dane's influence on the reform spirit in general was considerable, and although TR did not coin the term "muckraker" until 1906, Riis was clearly one of the first of that breed.

TIDBITS: ✪ *Most tenements had two apartments to a floor, connected by a narrow hallway; the resulting floor plan gave them the name "dumbbell tenements."* ✪ *Domestic economy, ca. 1890:*

A family of five on East 10th Street could bring in $45 a month rolling cigars. Monthly rent for two rooms was $12.25. ✪ *Other business, 1890: passage of the Sherman Anti-Trust Act.*

"Bury My Heart at Wounded Knee."
Wounded Knee massacre, 1890

In the same year that Jacob Riis was documenting the devastation of immigrants' lives in the New York slums, a Paiute Indian prophet called Wovoka was addressing a different kind of devastation on the Great Plains. By the 1880s, the government's "contain and conquer" policy had succeeded in crowding most of the formerly nomadic tribes into poorly administered reservations, where game was scarce, alcohol was plentiful, the soil was poor, and ancient religious practices were prohibited. In a visionary reaction to this living death, Wovoka began, around 1889, to preach a messianic "Ghost Dance" religion. If the Indian people took up the trancelike dance, he said, the country would miraculously be cleansed of white intruders, dead ancestors and slaughtered buffalo would return, and the old ways would be reborn in a fruitful land.

Wovoka's vision attracted wide attention, not only among the Indian peoples themselves, but also—fatefully, as it turned out—among Indian agents who feared the dancing would lead to warfare. The Bureau of Indian Affairs took the new religion seriously enough to suggest that the army curb it before it got out of hand, and in December 1890, that's what happened.

Since Sitting Bull's Hunkpapa Sioux were among Wovoka's most enthusiastic followers, the Seventh Cavalry—"martyred" Custer's outfit—attempted to arrest Sitting Bull. On December 15, in a fight between his followers and Indian police, he was killed. Two weeks later, a Sioux band led by Big Foot was on its way to Pine Ridge Reservation in South Dakota when the same regiment overtook it at Wounded Knee Creek and held it at gunpoint overnight. Big Foot's group contained perhaps three hundred people, about two-thirds of them women and children, while the surrounding soldiers numbered approximately five hundred and were armed with automatic Hotchkiss guns as well as carbines. The next morning, when the cavalry began to disarm the captive Indians, a shot rang out. Although nobody knew which side had fired, the Hotchkiss guns rattled fiercely in response for several minutes, leaving two hundred Indians dead in the snow. About thirty soldiers also lost their lives, some of them almost certainly by their own crossfire.

Described as the last "battle" of the Plains Indian wars, Wounded Knee was, in fact, even less a battle than the infamous Sand Creek Massacre of 1864. However, it was the last exchange of fire between the army and the Sioux. Poet Stephen Vincent Benét's touching line, "Bury my heart at Wounded Knee," reflects the poignancy of the event, and the phrase was adopted as a fitting title by Dee Brown for his 1971 "Indian History of the American West."

T I D B I T S : ✪ *Five years before his death, "troublemaker" Sitting Bull was touring the country with Buffalo Bill Cody's Wild West Show.* ✪ *Wounded Knee resurfaced in the news in 1973, when militant leaders of the American Indian Movement, outraged anew at debilitating government policies, staged a two-month occupation of Pine Ridge Reservation.*

"I Pledge Allegiance to the Flag . . ."

Pledge of Allegiance, 1892

You'd think this one would go way back, but it doesn't. A verbal salute to the American flag wasn't introduced until 1892, in response to President Benjamin Harrison's executive request that schools celebrate the four hundredth anniversary of Columbus's voyage. The original Pledge appeared in the juvenile magazine *Youth's Companion* that year and was probably written by editor Francis Bellamy. His wording went like this: "I pledge allegiance to my flag and to the Republic for which it stands, one Nation indivisible, with liberty and justice for all."

But you'll only remember it that way if you can also remember World War I. By 1923, as folks were trying to forget about Europe and enjoying the "normalcy" of Warren Harding's reign, the American Legion had advised replacing the ambiguous "my flag" with "the flag of the United States of America." That done, the Pledge remained unchanged until 1954, when Congress sought to check the creeping advance of Godless communism by adding the pious rider "under God." This irked the three or four actual atheists in the country and brought devotees of the ACLU out in droves, fearful that the mere mention of the dreaded "G" word would bring the separation of church and state rattling to the ground. The pro-God people prevailed, although every few years someone else tries to outlaw the mention of God as unconstitutional.

It's a pointless argument, considering that since 1943 no school district or public assembly has been able legally to require the speaking of the Pledge, in any form. In that year the Supreme Court struck down a West Virginia statute demanding recitation; since then, school flag salutes, like morning Bible readings, technically have been voluntary. So whatever the passions, the wording changes are moot.

Of course, whether it can legally be required or not, the Pledge of Allegiance has become as integral a part of patriotic display as the flag itself. So central is the traditional Pledge to "flag etiquette" that it gets a whole section in the congressionally approved flag code. That code, adopted in 1942, stipulates how the flag is to be raised, displayed, carried, draped, disposed of, and generally respected. Some of it makes for pretty interesting reading. Did you know, for example, that when the flag is suspended over a street, the blue field should be "to the north in an east and west street or to the east in a north and south street"? Or that the flag "should never be carried flat or horizontally, but always aloft and free"? Or that it should never be used as a ceiling covering? Me neither.

While some see such regulations as silly, others take them dead seriously. The two camps have clashed in recent years, most notably during the Vietnam War, when peaceniks displayed flags "disrespectfully" as articles of clothing; and again during the Iran hostage crisis, when Islamic revolutionaries burned the flag as a sign of outrage. Adopting that symbolically potent act, American radicals began to burn flags in the late 1980s. Congress took *them* seriously enough to debate a Constitutional amendment making flag-burning a federal offense. Section 4 of the flag code already stipulates that "no disrespect should be shown" to the flag; burning it was something the writers never even considered.

TIDBITS: ✪ *Kids Say the Darndest Things Department: "I like the Pledge, but who's this Richard Stands?"* ✪ *1990 bumper sticker: "Flag burners: If I see you burning the flag of my country, I will exercise my freedom of expression to adjust your attitude."* ✪ *Other news, 1892: Gentleman Jim Corbett defeats John L. Sullivan for the heavyweight boxing championship of the world.*

"You Shall Not Crucify Mankind Upon a Cross of Gold."

William Jennings Bryan, 1896

The Gay Nineties in American history were more than gay. The dance halls, nickel beers, and bouncy tunes were there, yes. But there was also the gravest class division the country had seen since the rise of Jacksonian democracy. In New York City and other cosmopolitan centers, millionaires like Diamond Jim Brady spent fortunes on single dinners, while Gotham social arbiter Ward McAllister coined the invidious phrase "The Four Hundred" to describe the number of people in New York high society. (Four hundred was the capacity of socialite Mrs. William Astor's ballroom.) At the same time, Jacob Riis was investigating the slums (see page 119), working people were fighting the century's deepest depression, and farmers were watching their holdings being put on the auction block daily.

Even before reckless speculation generated the fearful Panic of 1893, farmers had begun to organize against what they saw as conspiratorial money interests. In the 1892 national elections, they backed former Union general James B. Weaver on the Populist party ticket. To right the economic and social imbalance, the Populists called for low-interest loans, a progressive income tax, federal ownership of the hated railroads, direct election of U.S. senators, and—most dramatically—the free, unlimited coinage of silver. This last demand may have been more symbolic than pragmatic, but they proposed it with messianic gravity. "Free Silver" became the rallying cry of countless debtors who believed that the minting of more, and thus cheaper, money would be a remedy for their distress.

The Populists got a million votes but lost the election. The Panic hit almost as soon as Grover Cleveland took office, and for the next four years, economic matters worsened. In the spring of 1894, a wage cut at the Pullman railroad car company led to a massive strike and federal repression of the strikers; the ensuing resentment generated riots around the country. Meanwhile, Ohio businessman Jacob Coxey marched a small army of the unemployed on Washington, demanding the creation of public-works jobs and the printing of money. He was arrested for trespassing on the Capitol lawn.

With labor and farm unrest on the upswing, "Free Silver" dominated the 1896 election—a symbolic fight between the haves and have-nots. Probusiness Republicans nominated William McKinley, who supported a "hard money" gold standard and a protective tariff. The Democrats put forward Nebraska's William Jennings Bryan, the handsomely earnest "Boy Orator of the Platte." Bryan had already spoken out widely for Free Silver, and he brought down the house at the Chicago nominating convention when he raised a stentorian challenge to the Republicans: "You shall not press down upon the brow of labor this crown of thorns. You shall not crucify mankind upon a cross of gold."

Bryan absorbed the Populist vote and took 6.5 million popular votes in all, but he lost the election to the "safer" Republicans. Although he took twenty-two out of forty-five states, those states were far less thickly populated than McKinley's Northeast. This was eighty years before political clout shifted to the Sun Belt, and "the South and the desert," as Bryan's mockers put it, were not enough to give Bryan a mandate.

As president, McKinley established a protective tariff even higher than the 1890 one that bore his name, started America toward her destiny as world policeman, and fell to an assassin's bullet in 1901. Bryan lost two more presidential elections, served briefly as Woodrow Wilson's secretary of state, and defended the Bible in Tennessee's famous Monkey Trial (page 151). Free Silver fell out of the picture in 1900, when the nation officially adopted the gold standard.

"A Splendid Little War"

Spanish-American War, 1899

Being a world power means being able to manage other people's business when you think your national interest requires it—a distinction the United States achieved in 1899, when it clashed with Spain in what Secretary of State John Hay called "a splendid little war."

The trouble began in Cuba, which in 1895 revolted against Spanish rule. Expansionist Americans had been eyeing the sugar-rich island throughout the period of Manifest Destiny, and even the more isolationist minded, moved by commercial as well as humanitarian impulses, expressed strong sympathy with the insurgents. This sympathy was fed by a Spanish general, Valeriano Weyler, whose brutal responses to the rebels—incarcerating them in concentration camps, for example—earned him the nickname "Butcher." American newspaper publishers Joseph Pulitzer and William Randolph Hearst, then engaged in a circulation war, fanned the flames of outrage with sensationalist reporting, for which they earned the nickname "yellow journalists."

The yellow press did not hesitate to bend the rules of evidence or propriety when it might serve the cause of higher subscriptions. When one of Hearst's spies stole a letter in which the Spanish ambassador openly ridiculed President McKinley, Hearst ran it on the front page of his *New York Morning Journal*. When Cuba-based artist Frederic Remington wired that conditions weren't bad enough to justify a war, Hearst is reputed to have shot back, "You furnish the pictures and I'll furnish the war." So one of the drawings Remington sent back showed male Spanish officials strip-searching an American woman—a task the Spanish assigned to female attendants.

The biggest opportunity for boosting circulation came in February of 1898, when the American battleship *Maine* exploded in Havana harbor, sending 260 sailors to their deaths. In an era when "quality control" had not yet become a manufacturing buzzword, the logical culprit in the tragedy was a ruptured boiler—and that's exactly where a Spanish inspection team laid the blame. Cuban rebels, intent on drawing U.S. forces into the fray, might have run a close second. The *least* likely candidate was the Spanish government, which was desperately trying to prevent American involvement in the affair. But the Spanish it had to have been, according to Hearst. After his *Journal* and its rivals ran banner headlines pleading with Americans to "Remember the Maine," in late April President McKinley went to war.

The conflict, which lasted less than four months, provided more than its share of folklore. The hero of the Far East campaign, George Dewey, became the navy's first five-star admiral, and a presidential hopeful, after destroying the Spanish fleet in Manila Bay; his comment "You may fire when you are ready, Gridley" (see page 232), remains a pithy staple of armed-services memory. After an equally swift victory in the Caribbean, Admiral William Sampson grandly cabled Washington, presenting the Spanish fleet to the nation as a Fourth of July present. And in Cuba itself, a colorful gallimaufry of Eastern playboys and Western cowboys known as the Rough Riders took San Juan Hill away from Spanish defenders, bringing their spunky commander, Teddy Roosevelt, to national prominence.

When a treaty was signed at the end of the year, the United States acquired the former Spanish possessions of Puerto Rico, Guam, and the Philippines in exchange for a payment of $20 million. Although Cuba was released from Spanish control, it was tied reluctantly to its northern liberator by the Platt Amendment three years later. By requiring American approval for any of Cuba's international agreements, it made the island, in effect, a U.S. protectorate. Thus at one stroke the United States strengthened its Monroe Doctrine privileges and became a player in the international real-estate scramble.

The inevitable management problems became painfully apparent in 1899, when the Philippines revolted against their new masters. President McKinley, originally opposed to acquiring them, had gone along in the hope that American control would eventually "uplift and civilize" the islands' inhabitants. When the revolt was finally quelled in 1902, with great loss of life, anti-imperialist Andrew Carnegie wrote to a U.S. government official, "You seem to have about finished your work of civilizing the Filipinos. About eight thousand of them have been completely civilized and sent to Heaven. I hope you like it."

While Carnegie and a few others might complain, the majority of Americans liked it fine. The "splendid little war" thrust the country onto the world stage. It earned respect for American fiber and American arms. Not least of all, it provided a tonic for embittered spirits: the economic turmoil of the preceding decade was temporarily forgotten as embattled workers, like everyone else, followed the flag. The formula would not be used with such effectiveness until the liberation of Kuwait a century later.

TIDBITS : ✪ *Joseph Pulitzer funded the Pulitzer Prizes.* ✪ *Hearst was the model for Orson Welles's* Citizen Kane *and the grandfather of "heiress bandit" Patty Hearst.* ✪ *"Yellow" came from the fact that the Hearst and Pulitzer papers both carried the pioneering comic strip "The Yellow Kid."* ✪ *TR actually was the Rough Riders' second in command. Their commander, Brigadier General Leonard Wood, later governed both Cuba and the Philippines.* ✪ *U.S. forces lost slightly more than five thousand men in the Spanish-American War, more than 90 percent of them to tropical disease.*

"Open Door"

John Hay, 1899

When Japan took Korea away from China in the Sino-Japanese War (1894–95), the Western powers were put on notice that the inscrutable East was also a player in the imperialist chess game, and that even their own economic spheres of influence might be threatened by an expansionist Tokyo regime. Accordingly the Europeans, who had just cozily carved Africa up among themselves, started doing the same thing to China, much to the distress of British merchants, who had dominated Chinese trade for half a century. To save as much of the market as possible for itself, Britain appealed to the United States in 1898 to endorse an equal-access policy toward the Far East.

Good idea, bad timing. The Americans in that year, you will remember, were engaged in carving out their own spheres of influence by wresting sugar-rich Cuba and sundry other islands from the Spanish. The initial response to the British proposal was, therefore, a polite rebuff. A year later, however, with the Spanish acquisitions comfortably engorged, the United States reconsidered. In September 1899, Secretary of State John Hay, fresh from his "splendid little war," sent a note around to all the great powers reproposing the British idea: If we are going to tap the Chinese market niche, it said, we should all get an equal shot at the pickings. That is, no exclusive spheres of influence—and no tariffs keeping U.S. merchants out. The "Open Door" attitude implicit here defined the Americans' China policy until World War II.

Hay's offer wasn't accepted with whoops of joy, but it was accepted. Italy, who had nothing to lose because she *had* no Chinese sphere of influence, said, "What a great idea." France, Germany, Japan, and beleaguered Britain all said, "We'll do it if the others will." Only Russia, which had its eyes on China's western province of Manchuria, responded with a polite "No thanks." But China itself—which had not been consulted on the matter and resented foreigners in any combination—broke out in violence over the affair. In 1900, a nationalist secret society, the Boxers, began killing foreigners and besieging their legations. In response, the Western powers, along with Japan, formed a coalition of eighteen thousand troops, and they soon put down the so-called Boxer Rebellion.

The outcome, not so ironically, entrenched Hay's policy. He issued a codicil to the original Open Door note, proclaiming China's territorial integrity (on paper) while foreign troops set up posts not only in Peking, but along the principal cargo highway, the Yangtze River. The allies also demanded reparations: $333 million in all, about $24 million for U.S. losses alone.

In an uncharacteristically nonmercenary gesture, America later gave three-quarters of this payment back, to be used for educating Chinese students in the United States. This last fillip to the "opening" of China helped to create a pro-American Chinese managerial class that in years to come would keep the trade wheels humming smoothly.

TIDBITS: ✪ *Hay's other claims to fame: he had been Abraham Lincoln's private secretary throughout the war years, wrote a massive Lincoln biography, and in 1903 drafted the treaty acquir-*

ing access rights for the land that would become the Panama Canal Zone. ✪ *"Boxer" was a slang condensation. A more literal translation would have been "The Society of Harmonious, Righteous Fists."*

"That Damned Cowboy"

Mark Hanna, 1901

After an assassin's bullet killed Republican kingmaker Marcus Hanna's protégé, William McKinley, Hanna delivered this classic I-told-you-so to party regulars: "Now look. That damned cowboy is president of the United States." A staunch proponent of McKinley's protective tariff and of probusiness legislation in general, the Ohio senator had fought Teddy Roosevelt's place on the 1900 ticket because he feared the former Rough Rider's unpredictability, and specifically his lack of affection for corporate interests. Personally as well as politically, McKinley's death was for Hanna a "one-heartbeat-away-from-the-White-House" nightmare-come-true.

The nightmare didn't turn out to be as bad as Hanna had expected, but it certainly rattled the probusiness complacency of the McKinley years. One year after moving into the White House, Roosevelt ended a miners' strike by threatening the mine owners with federal intervention. The following year, he got Congress to establish a Department of Commerce and Labor that would investigate abuses by the nation's trusts. "Trust busting" soon became an administration priority, as Theodore Roosevelt attacked railroad bribery and rebates; outlawed monopolies in the beef, sugar, and fertilizer industries; and—reacting to muckraking exposés—pushed through a Pure

Food and Drug Act to protect consumers. In his most famous victory against "combination," he used the Sherman Anti-Trust Act, a toothless tiger since 1890, to dissolve J. P. Morgan's vast holding company, the Northern Securities Company.

His reputation aside, however, Roosevelt moved less precipitously than Hanna might have feared. While denouncing the bad apples—whom he called "certain malefactors of great wealth"—he recognized just as well as Hanna the role bigness played in the American economic system, and his tenure actually saw the *formation* of more trusts than had the administration of corporate lapdog William McKinley. In addition, Theodore Roosevelt's successor, the ostensibly conservative William Howard Taft, mounted *twice* as many antitrust suits in four years as the Rough Rider had pulled off in more than seven. The nation's premier political humorist, Finley Peter Dunne, had it about right when he had his indomitable Irish pundit, "Mr. Dooley," give this summary of TR's views on giant businesses: "On wan hand I wud stamp thim undher fut; on th' other hand not so fast."

While his blustery, indefatigable personal style could hardly be termed moderate, moderate is not a bad description of Roosevelt's domestic policies. Running for reelection in 1903, he promised first veterans, and then everybody else, a "square deal." That sense of balance won him the office in 1904 against the forgettable Alton B. Parker and (in the first of four presidential tries) the Socialist hero Eugene V. Debs. Hanna, who had hoped to unseat Roosevelt himself as the Republican candidate, died a few months before the party convention.

TIDBITS: ✪ *When Hanna's political management got McKinley elected the first time in 1896, Roosevelt commented that McKinley had been sold to the public "like a patent medicine." This was seventy years before writer Joe McGinniss, in his unsettling book* The Selling of the President, *made substantially the same point about Richard Nixon.* ✪ *TR's "square deal" promise started a trend. His cousin FDR came out with a "new" deal, and his successor, Harry Truman, offered a "fair" one. All three promised support for the "forgotten man."*

"Speak Softly and Carry a Big Stick."

Theodore Roosevelt, 1901

Teddy Roosevelt thought of this line as a personal motto, but he also made it a guiding principle for his administration. Critics have spied its intrusion everywhere, from the president's trust-busting to his supposed disdain for the Constitution, but today the "Big Stick" is most commonly thought of as a definition for Roosevelt's foreign-policy stance.

When Roosevelt took office, in 1901, the United States had just acquired its first overseas possessions as a result of its "splendid little war" (see page 127) with the Spanish empire. TR had shone there himself in a military capacity, and his attitude toward the nation's emerging power was one of unbridled pride and bristling enthusiasm. He welcomed the responsibilities of being a world leader and twice played peacemaker in international conflicts. In 1905, in Portsmouth, New Hampshire, he hosted a conference between Russian and Japanese emissaries that ended a year-old war between their two countries. The following year he defused a clash over Morocco by defending France's claim against the German Kaiser's. For these efforts, he won the Nobel Peace Prize—just before he sent a "Great White Fleet" of warships around the world in a three-year show of American naval power.

But it was his home waters that he stirred most forcefully with the Big Stick. In one celebrated example of his "cowboy diplomacy," he supported (some would say created) a 1903 revolution in Colombia, freeing land in breakaway Panama for the digging of "our" canal. Later that year he established a naval base in Cuba's Guantánamo Bay, and in 1906 (the year of the Peace Prize), he landed Marines on the island to put down an insurrection. Interventions in the Dominican Republic and in Venezuela further signaled U.S. hegemony in the region. In 1904 TR had formalized his intrusiveness in the so-called Roosevelt Corollary to the Monroe Doctrine—making the United States, in effect, the region's policeman—but even without that document, it was obvious that the Caribbean was becoming an "American lake."

Roosevelt's successor, three-hundred-pound William Howard Taft, tried to replace the Big Stick with the Big Checkbook by encouraging bankers to invest strategically in foreign economies, especially in the recently "opened" Far East and in the Caribbean. This dollar diplomacy was supposed to solidify American interests while keeping European money and influence out of the picture, but it never really got off the ground. In the East, the Russians and Japanese nixed a U.S. plan to buy their Manchurian railroad lines for the Chinese, and along the "American lake," discontent in Nicaragua forced our corpulent captain to send in the Marines to protect the very money that was supposed to have created stability.

Taft's successor, the anti-imperialist Woodrow Wilson, fared no better. The Big Stick seemed to be stuck to his hand against his will, as he too sent troops into the Caribbean and, in 1916, into northern Mexico in a vain attempt to capture rebel Pancho Villa. Since Wilson's day the nation's "south of the border" diplomacy has combined elements of TR's brusqueness and Taft's "investment," in the process entrenching the view of the Yankee patron as a sometimes helpful, but often venal, outside meddler.

✪ *Most frequent beneficiary of our "benevolent" intrusion: Nicaragua, invaded three times between 1909 and 1933 (four if you count Mr. Reagan's Contras).* ✪ *Most durable Big Stick outpost: the U.S. naval base at Guantánamo Bay, which has survived nearly four decades of Fidel Castro's rule.* ✪ *Biggest Big Stick blunder: John F. Kennedy's failed invasion of Cuba at the Bay of Pigs in 1961.*

Muckrakers

Theodore Roosevelt, 1906

By the last decades of the nineteenth century, Americans were becoming painfully aware that the social progress on which they prided themselves suffered from serious shortcomings and flagrant abuses. Beginning in the 1870s—the heyday of the corrupt Grant administration—a literature of protest began to call attention to these abuses, making "reform" an indispensable part of the politician's vocabulary. In 1879, maverick economist Henry George denounced landlords' "unearned income" in *Progress and Poverty.* Two years later, in the *Atlantic Monthly,* Henry Demarest Lloyd set the stage for Teddy Roosevelt's "trust busting" with an exposé of the Standard Oil Company. In 1888, Edward Bellamy's best-selling novel *Looking Backward* questioned the validity of the free-enterprise system itself, and in 1890, New York reporter Jacob Riis shone a spotlight on slum conditions in *How the Other Half Lives.* Three years after that, editor S. S. McClure founded a magazine that attacked shortcomings in every aspect of public life and provided a forum for progressive social analysts.

What we today call the muckraking movement is usually

traced to the November 1902 issue of *McClure's*, in which investigative reporter Ida Tarbell began a series of exposés of Standard Oil—a corporate giant she didn't like any better than Lloyd had. Following Tarbell came a flurry of finger-pointing toward other such trusts. Articles appeared in *McClure's* and a host of rival magazines, including such conservative ones as *Ladies' Home Journal*, and in the first ten years of the century, approximately a thousand such features hit the stands.

Many of them grew into books. Lincoln Steffens's *The Shame of the Cities* (1904) linked civic graft to standard industrial practices, and Thomas Lawson's *Frenzied Finance* (1905) attacked stock manipulation. Samuel Hopkins Adams's *The Great American Fraud* (1906) exposed the patent medicine industry, while Ray Stannard Baker's *Following the Color Line* (1908) documented racial injustice. Even novelists got into the act, with Frank Norris attacking the railroads in *The Octopus* (1901) and Upton Sinclair taking on the meat industry in *The Jungle* (1906).

President Teddy Roosevelt, in spite of his own commitment to reform, feared the "extremism" of such writing as socially disruptive and, ironically enough, was responsible for giving the movement its unsavory nickname. (At least *he* thought it was unsavory; the muckrakers themselves wore it as a badge of honor.) This happened in 1906, when he likened radical writers to a character in *Pilgrim's Progress*. In John Bunyan's allegory, the "man with the Muck-rake" ignores the "Celestial Crown" that he is offered in exchange for the tool, preferring to attend exclusively to "the Straws, the small Sticks, and Dust of the Floor."

Muckraking proper ended just before World War I, but its spirit lives on today. Consumer activist Ralph Nader has followed a muckraking faith for a quarter-century, ever since his 1965 exposé of the auto industry; *Washington Post* reporters Bob Woodward and Carl Bernstein, in bringing the Watergate scandal to light, were working in the tradition of Lincoln Steffens; while tabloid journalism, whether of the print or electronic variety, sustains the sensationalist bias—if not always the moral zeal—of the muckraking era. If *McClure's* has heirs, they are *Mother Jones* and "60 Minutes."

TIDBITS: ✪ *In the 1870s, before reformist courts started to break it up, John D. Rockefeller's Standard Oil controlled 90 percent of U.S. oil refining.* ✪ *Ida Tarbell's best-known book is her 1904 history of Standard Oil; in a lesser-known gem, the 1916* New Ideals for Business, *she praises the "productivity through people" approach of progressive firms.*

The Wisconsin Idea

*Robert La Follette and Progressivism,
ca. 1900–1915*

During the Progressive Era, the federal government made concerted efforts to mute the influence of traditional power brokers such as industry lobbyists and party hacks, and strove to empower traditionally weak groups such as laborers, children, and women. The spurs for such aptly named "progressive" legislation were the needling exposés of the muckrakers, but its prototypes were laws passed in reform-minded state houses, mostly in the West and Midwest. To a great extent the national reform spirit followed the lead of these pioneering state legislatures.

Women's suffrage, for example, became national law only in 1920, with the ratification of the Nineteenth Amendment. Yet Wyoming had granted women the vote in 1869, and by the 1890s three other western states—Colorado, Idaho, and

Utah—had followed suit. The first federal workmen's compensation law came in 1908, six years after Maryland's state version. The first effective national regulation of the railroads, the 1906 Hepburn Act, followed by a year Wisconsin's establishment of a state railroad regulatory commission. And while the direct election of U.S. senators became federal law with the Seventeenth Amendment of 1913, a decade earlier saw both Oregon and Wisconsin establish the direct primary for state officials.

Oregon and Wisconsin were the most ambitious in their Progressive designs. Under the so-called Oregon System, which began in 1902, voters could use the initiative, referendum, and recall to influence the activities of their elected officials. In Wisconsin—which under Governor Bob La Follette and his successors was virtually a Camelot of Progressive ideas—voters got not only the direct primary and worker's compensation laws, but utility regulation, a pioneering minimum wage, tax reform, an anticorruption act, liberal pensions, statewide vocational training—and even the first kindergartens in the country.

As many of these reforms were adopted by the La Follette government after consultation with University of Wisconsin professors, such an academic-legislative link became known as the Wisconsin Idea. The idea has resurfaced, albeit with modifications, in various presidential administrations. FDR's New Deal "brain trust," JFK's reliance on Harvard faculty members, Ronald Reagan's deference to University of Chicago economic theorists—all may be seen as variations of the Wisconsin Idea.

La Follette was elected governor three times, then served as U.S. senator from 1906 until his death in 1925. His greatest national prominence came in 1924, when he ran for president on the Progressive party ticket. With strong labor and farm support he took 17 percent of the popular vote, but he lost to the safer, if duller, Calvin Coolidge.

"The World Must Be Made Safe for Democracy."

Woodrow Wilson, April 2, 1917

Elected on a peace platform in 1916, Wilson was desperate to keep his country out of the Great War in spite of numerous provocations by German U-boats. Even after the torpedoed British passenger ship *Lusitania* sank with more than one hundred Americans on board in 1915, the president managed to keep his own and the nation's composure; as late as January 1917, when he delivered his famous "Peace without Victory" speech (see page 144) to Congress, he still hoped the Europeans would settle it themselves. The speech, which warned that only a "peace between equals" could last, was clearly a noncombatant's contribution. On the last day of that month, however, his patience broke, when Germany announced that the supposed "restraint" it had been showing with regard to neutral shipping was officially, as of that date, at an end. The resumption of unrestricted submarine warfare would now make American merchantmen, whatever their cargo, torpedo targets.

After that, things developed quickly. In February the German ambassador was asked to leave town, relations with his country were officially severed, and British spies gave our spies an intercepted message in which Germany solicited support from our neighbor Mexico in exchange for backing a Mexican reconquest of the American Southwest. Printed in the U.S. papers on March 1, the so-called Zimmermann note was a heavy blow to the president's hopes. When later that month three U.S. cargo ships were sent to the bottom by the Kaiser's U-boats, Wilson had had enough, and on April 2 he asked for a declaration of war.

The language in which Wilson made this request was typically sententious. He referred to the U-boats as "outlaws" against the freedom of the seas and noted that the self-defensive "armed neutrality" the United States was following had, by Germany's action, been rendered "impractical." He didn't mention that our vessels were carrying the Allies arms and supplies—or that the German attacks were principally designed to halt this flow. Indeed, rather than debate with the Germans on the pros and cons of unimpeded commerce, he chose to suggest, eloquently, that their submarine policy constituted a "warfare against mankind."

Since the U-boats had targeted clearly marked hospital and relief ships, "inhumanity" was an easy note to sound, and Wilson made the most of the opportunity. Asking the country to "formally accept the status of belligerent which has thus been thrust upon it," he made a case for active American involvement. Displaying as much fervor for war as he had over the years for peace, he called Germany a "natural foe to liberty" and claimed, in the speech's most remembered line, that "the world must be made safe for democracy."

"We are but one of the champions of the rights of mankind," Wilson intoned in words that would have delighted the Founding Fathers. "Our object . . . is to vindicate the principles of peace and justice in the life of the world as against selfish and autocratic power and to set up amongst the really free and self-governed peoples of the world such a concert of purpose and of action as will henceforth insure the observance of those principles." In thus equating victory for the Allied cause with the expansion of democratic principles, Wilson transformed an unwelcome burden into a sacred duty.

It was a great speech, and four days later Wilson got his declaration. Two months after that, the first doughboys boarded their troopships. After three years of trying to keep clear of Europe's tragedy, America was finally going "over there."

TIDBITS: ✪ *By-the-Way Department: The speech also called for the military conscription of half a million men. The Selective Service Act was passed one month later.* ✪ *"Over There," written by George M. Cohan, was the monster hit of 1917–18. Wilson called it "a genuine inspiration to all American manhood."*

"Lafayette, We Are Here."

Charles Stanton, 1917

In the War for Independence, French assistance had been crucial to America's victory, and no figure better symbolized the amity between the two nations than George Washington's friend and fellow officer, the popular young Marquis de Lafayette. Not only had he cheered bedraggled troops during the Continentals' bitter winter at Valley Forge, but he had raised needed money for the patriot cause (including $200,000 from his own pocket), and he had been present at the final victory at Yorktown. Therefore, when the United States entered World War I on the side of the Allies (Britain, France, and Russia), the sense of a debt being paid was inescapable. Charles Stanton's proud announcement at the marquis's Paris tomb acknowledged the debt—and the payment.

Given the small number of Americans actually in France that summer, the announcement was a little premature. Stanton, a colonel attached to General John Pershing's American Expeditionary Forces, made his comment, appropriately enough, on the Fourth of July. A tiny group of American volunteer flyers—the famous Lafayette Escadrille—had been helping the French since the spring of 1916. But even though the home front was merrily humming George M. Cohan's "Over There," U.S. forces had just started to trickle in, with the first division having arrived only a week before. The American draft was barely off the ground, and it wasn't until late in October—six months after President Wilson's declaration of war—that our doughboys were in the trenches beside the French.

To be fair, when they did get into it, their help was critical in turning the tide. Initially as detachments to Allied forces, then as self-contained U.S. units, American soldiers figured dramatically in the last year's battles. In June 1918 they pushed the Germans back at Belleau Wood. The following month they halted the German advance along the Marne. In September more than half a million doughboys battled for St. Mihiel, taking sixteen thousand German soldiers prisoner. And in the last great engagement of the war, the Meuse-Argonne offensive, 1.2 million Americans played a part. It was that battle's victory that ended the war on November 11.

Although U.S. forces had been "over there" for less than a year and a half, they paid a heavy price for their nation's involvement. Approximately four million Yanks went into uniform. Of these, about 130,000 never came back—half of them battlefield casualties, the other half stricken by disease. For the combatants of other countries, the tolls were, of course, higher. The British lost 900,000 young men on the battlefield alone, and France close to 1.4 million. The most severely devastated nations were the Kaiser's Germany, with 1.6 million deaths at the front, and Russia, newly sovietized, with 1.7 million. With good reason historians speak of the Great War as having decimated an entire civilization. When Gertrude Stein spoke of the "Lost Generation," she was referring to the shell-shocked emptiness left in the wake of World War I.

TIDBITS: ✪ *Lafayette's given name: Marie-Joseph-Paul-Yves-Roch-Gilbert du Motier.* ✪ *Charles Stanton was the nephew of Edwin M. Stanton, Lincoln's troublesome secretary of war.* ✪ *Most celebrated hero of the Argonne: U.S. Sergeant Alvin C. York, who captured 132 Germans single-handedly. In the Hollywood version, director Howard Hawks's* Sergeant York, *the quiet hero is played by Gary Cooper.*

Fourteen Points

Woodrow Wilson, January 1918

Ten months before the Great War ended, President Wilson went before Congress to propose a victor's menu for the settlement of the peace. An Allied conference had recently failed to agree upon an armistice formula, and Russia was starting to sound out the Kaiser for a separate peace, so there was a certain degree of urgency in the matter. The Fourteen Points that the ex-professor put forward as the "only possible" postwar program reiterated the principles of international cooperation laid down in the famous "Peace without Victory" speech that he had given a year before. In that speech he had called for "peace between equals," "government by the consent of the governed," freedom of the seas, and arms reduction. The Fourteen Points went beyond this call in several particulars. The first five spoke to general concerns:

I. "Open covenants of peace, openly arrived at." Clearly targeted toward Russia, this indicated that the United States would not accept "private understandings" between nations.

II. "Absolute freedom of navigation upon the seas." This went back to the troubled days of 1812, although it referred more immediately to the German U-boat menace.

III. The removal of "economic barriers" and the establishment of "equality of trade conditions." This piece of Wilsonian idealism didn't bear fruit until the 1950s, when the European Common Market was established.

IV. Reduction of armaments to "the lowest point consistent with domestic safety." (If anyone had been able to determine what that point was, there might not have been a Great War in the first place.)

V. Adjustment of colonial claims, taking into consideration "the interests of the populations concerned." In other words, the great powers should ask the people of their overseas territories if they wanted to be colonized at all. This ancient knot only started to unravel after the national liberation movements following the *second* World War.

The next eight points addressed the warring parties' land claims, proposing such high-minded but unworkable guidelines as "historically established lines of allegiance and nationality" in the resetting of postwar boundary lines. Specifically, Wilson said that occupying armies should leave Russia and Belgium; that Alsace-Lorraine should go back to the French; that territorial integrity should be assured for Italy, Austria-Hungary, Turkey, and the Balkans; and that the long-suffering Poles should get their own nation. The nuts and bolts of Wilson's "readjustment" dream, Points VI through XIII constituted a pretty fair-minded, although not entirely successful, approach to border wrangling.

The last point, and the most famous, read like this: "A general association of nations must be formed under specific covenants for the purpose of affording mutual guarantees of political independence and territorial integrity to great and small states alike." Point XIV was thus the genesis of the League of Nations, the international body that obsessed Wilson after the war, and that eventually led to his party's defeat in 1920.

One week before the German surrender, the Allies accepted the Fourteen Points in principle as the basis of the peace, demurring only on Point II, freedom of the seas. Since America had entered the war in the first place to defend that freedom, such Allied resistance did not bode well for future discussions. And in the peace settlement signed at Versailles in June 1919, the European victors proved themselves capable of precisely the vindictiveness Wilson had warned against. While much of the Fourteen Point program was adopted, the Allies imposed such penalties on beaten Germany that a sense of injustice, and a lust for revenge on the part of the Germans, were virtually assured.

The American people, stung into isolationism by their brief, bloody involvement in the Great War, came to reject both the League of Nations *and* the Versailles agreement, calling for a return to "normalcy" with Warren Gamaliel Harding. The League itself, hindered by the same lack of muscle that has often impeded its successor, the United Nations, managed to settle various border disputes in the 1920s and 1930s, but it was powerless against Italian expansionism under Mussolini and fell apart in the aftermath of World War II.

T I D B I T S : ✪ *The Allied "Big Four" at Versailles were Wilson, France's Georges Clemenceau, Great Britain's David Lloyd George, and Italy's Vittorio Orlando.* ✪ *Although his dreams for international cooperation were rejected at home, Wilson was able to console himself with the 1919 Nobel Peace Prize.*

Suffragettes

Nineteenth Amendment, adopted 1920

The "other 50 percent" of the U.S. population finally got the right to vote more than seventy years after Elizabeth Cady Stanton and Lucretia Mott convened the Seneca Falls Convention (1848) to discuss the gender-based double standards of their time. The two women had been denied admission to a London antislavery convention in 1840; spying hypocrisy, they turned to fighting covert—as well as open—slavery. To Stanton this meant working not only for equal educational and work opportunities for women, but also for their "sacred right to the elective franchise." Mott originally balked at this proposal, saying, "Lizzie, thee will make us ridiculous," but she went along, and the Seneca Falls meeting adopted a suffrage agenda.

The Civil War put a hold on women's suffrage, but in 1869 the issue was raised again, when Stanton and Susan B. Anthony formed the National Women's Suffrage Association. In 1872 Anthony voted illegally in a Rochester, New York, election. Fined $100, she refused to cough it up, saying she was willing to ignore any law in order to "protect an enslaved woman." That same year, free-love advocate Victoria Woodhull ran for president on the Equal Rights ticket—to less than cheers from her more conservative colleagues. This period also saw the publication of the first feminist journals, Stanton's *Revolution* (1868) and Lucy Stone's more benignly titled *Women's Journal* (1870).

Stone, who had founded the American Women's Suffrage Association in 1869, joined forces with Stanton and Anthony in 1890 to form the National American Women's Suffrage Association. Under this bulkily monikered umbrella, women struggled for voting rights for the next three decades, enduring heckling, physical abuse, and numerous arrests while managing

to drive a thin wedge into the system at the state level. Progressive Wyoming had given women the vote in 1869. By the 1896 elections, Colorado, Utah, and Idaho had followed suit. And in 1912 the issue had achieved enough prominence that Teddy Roosevelt's Bull Moose party endorsed "ballots for both."

The final push for national recognition came in the teens, with a militant physician, Alice Paul, burning effigies of President Wilson in the streets while Anthony's successor as NAWSA president, Carrie Chapman Catt, lobbied doggedly behind the scenes for a constitutional amendment. The dream was realized in 1919, when Congress narrowly passed the Nineteenth Amendment. It was ratified by the required states the following year, and women voted for the first time in a national election in which the winning slogan was, ironically, "Back to Normalcy."

Having achieved their primary objective, politicized women turned to a variety of other reforms in the years that followed. Spurred by author Betty Friedan, whose 1963 book, *The Feminine Mystique*, was the calling card of the modern women's liberation movement, activists have concentrated increasingly on legal issues ranging from job discrimination and "domestic slavery" to the availability of abortion. The strongest political arm of today's feminists is the National Organization for Women (founded 1966), but divergent groups have also surfaced. In the 1960s Radicalesbians and the Women's International Terrorist Conspiracy from Hell (WITCH) urged a complete break—physical and emotional—from society's "patriarchal" order. More recently, Feminists for Life, stressing the "interdependence of all living things," have called NOW's abortion-rights agenda a reactionary "capitulation to male convenience."

TIDBITS: ✪ *Stanton, who managed to raise seven children, also struck out the "obey" clause in her marriage vows.* ✪ *Lucy Stone kept her maiden name after marriage: hence "Lucy Stoner"*

for a woman who does the same. ✪ *Catt's second great contribution to women's rights: founding the League of Women Voters in 1920.*

The Roaring Twenties
1918–29

If wars begin with impassioned organization, they frequently end in disorganized passion. That historical truism is nowhere more obvious than in the rage for sensation that followed World War I. Some refer to that wild decade as the Jazz Age; others prefer the more calendrical Roaring Twenties. By any name it was a season of frenzied spirits who were running desperately to escape the memory of a shattered civilization.

The twenties meant short skirts and long nights. It meant "jazz" in both the musical and erotic senses, as flappers danced the Charleston and the Black Bottom and as "wild youth," newly tuned in to Dr. Freud's pronouncements, threw their parents' Victorian strictures to the winds. It meant an appreciation for outrageous excess in entertainment, whether it was flagpole-sitter Shipwreck Kelly in an aerial marathon, heavyweight champion Jack Dempsey drawing the first million-dollar sports gate, or the fabulous Babe Ruth cracking sixty homers. Most of all, it meant hooch and rum-running as the entire nation, officially dry, took up drinking.

That the greatest alcoholic spree in the country's history should have happened during Prohibition was, as William Blake might have pointed out, no more than the inevitable consequence of a stupid law. A greater irony was the fact that Prohibition, which temperance societies had been pushing for a hundred years, came about not as a result of their moral persuasion, but because World War I put a premium on distillable grains. As the Anti-Saloon League liked to point out, every bushel of rye converted into whiskey was a bushel that might have made bread for hungry doughboys. Such insights led to the 1917 Lever Act, which cut off grain supplies to the nation's distillers, and a few months later to the Eighteenth Amendment, which banned the sale or manufacture of "intoxicating liquors." The amendment went into effect in 1919, with state ratification and the passage of the Volstead Act, which put the feds in charge of keeping the country dry.

That the law was unenforceable was instantly obvious. Almost as soon as it was prohibited, drinking became the smart thing to do. Corner saloons may have been put out of business, but private clubs took over and then some: in New York City, an estimated fifteen thousand legal taverns gave way to about twice that many illegal speakeasies. Homemade and sometimes toxic "bathtub gin" became a less chic diversion, with more than a few suffering blindness as a result. Battles between bootleggers and federal officers became part of the country's folklore, especially in Appalachia and along the nation's coastlines. The law was mocked to a greater degree than it was observed—from the lowest to the highest levels of society. It was an open secret, for example, that President Harding tippled daily in the White House.

Inevitably, the sleaze factor grew as entrepreneurs with more moxie than morals muscled in. Raoul Walsh's grimly evocative tribute to the era, *The Roaring Twenties*, depicts gangsters as the driving force of Prohibition's economy, and that's not off the mark. Mr. Average American might have been content with home brew, but for the smart set, smuggled quality was more in order, and the underworld was perfectly happy to oblige. The birth of seriously organized crime in this country is a lasting legacy of the Prohibition era. As the decade's most notorious mobster, Chicago's Alphonse "Scarface" Capone, put it, "All I ever did was to sell whiskey to our best people."

"The Monkey Trial"

July 10–21, 1925

By the third decade of the twentieth century, Charles Darwin's theory of evolution, first proposed in 1859, had been taught in American schools for a generation. With the religious intensities of the Victorian era a distant memory, you might have thought that in 1925 nobody would care about a high-school teacher expounding this well-worn idea to his students. You would be wrong. In January of that year, responding to fundamentalist fears that the Bible was being ridiculed in the nation's classrooms, a Tennessee legislator named John Washington Butler proposed the banning of evolution theory from his state's schools. Passed in March, his bill was immediately put to a test in a courtroom trial that made that summer the most entertaining in Tennessee history.

The defendant in the case was a high-school biology teacher, John Thomas Scopes, who challenged the law with considerable help from the ACLU and the world-renowned Clarence Darrow as his chief attorney. The state prosecutor accepted the aid of an equally famous orator: the 1896 Democratic candidate for president, William Jennings Bryan. For eleven days in the Dayton, Tennessee, county courthouse, these two giants faced off against each other, Darrow defending Scopes's right to teach evolution on the grounds of both constitutionality and "reasonableness," Bryan citing the newly ratified Butler law as well as the law of God to claim that "blasphemy" was not, and should not be, part of the curriculum.

Even though the judge ruled irrelevant any evidence regarding the validity of Darwin's theory, that quickly became the trial's not-so-hidden agenda, as "descent from the apes" surfaced again and again in the proceedings. H. L. Mencken, one of dozens of reporters covering the case for the national media, gave it the felicitous tag "the monkey trial," and there was plenty of monkey business on the streets of Dayton. Lemonade stands shared sidewalk space with performing chimpanzees, and, as Scopes himself recalled in a 1966 memoir: "Merchants used monkey motifs in their advertising. Store windows featured little cotton apes. They sold pins that read, 'Your Old Man's a Monkey.' Robinson's Drugstore sold a Monkey Fizz, and a simian watch fob could be bought for sixty-five cents."

In addition, every crazy from a thousand miles around descended on the Tennessee hamlet to peddle his own theory. Soapboxes were nearly as thick as the dragonflies, and if you got tired of watching the chimps or perusing bookstalls with titles like *Hell and the High Schools* and *God or Gorilla*, you could listen to Wilber Glenn Voliva explain why the earth was flat, or Lewis Levi Johnson Marshall tell you why he was "the Absolute Ruler of the Entire World." Celebrity trials today—Zsa Zsa Gabor's, Roxanne Pulitzer's, Claus von Bulow's—are often turned into media circuses. They had nothing on the Clarence and Willy show.

In the high point of the trial, Darrow put his opposite number on the stand, grilling him mercilessly about his ignorance of both biblical and scientific data. Citing Archbishop James Ussher's famous pronouncement that the earth was created in 4004 B.C., for example, he needled Bryan into a posture of rank unreflectiveness by asking him how this figure was arrived at. "I never made a calculation," Bryan said. "A calculation from what?" "I could not say." "From the generations of man?" "I would not want to say that." "What do you *think?*" pushed on Darrow, theatrically exasperated. And a flustered Bryan shot back idiotically, "I do not think about things that I do not think about."

Local anti-evolutionist sentiment was so strong that, in spite of this poor prosecutorial showing, Scopes lost the case and was fined $100. The fine was voided by an appeals court on a technicality—fines above fifty bucks had to be imposed by a jury—and Scopes left teaching to become a geologist. Bryan died in bed five days after his hollow victory. Thus passed, in Scopes's generous estimation, "the most outstanding public speaker" the country had ever produced.

T I D B I T S : ✪ *Darrow's other famous clients: labor leader Eugene Debs, tried for contempt (1894); boy murderers Leopold and Loeb (1924).* ✪ *Hollywood's version of the trial, Stanley Kramer's superb* Inherit the Wind *(1960), stars Frederic March as Bryan, Spencer Tracy as Darrow, and Dick York as Scopes.* ✪ *It-Ain't-Over-Till-It's-Over Department: Butler's law stayed on the books until 1967.*

Sacco and Vanzetti

Anarchist "martyrs," executed 1927

The most famous example of Red-baiting in recent memory is the "witch-hunting" of Senator Joseph McCarthy (see page 182). But socialism has been frightening upwardly mobile Americans for 150 years, and well before McCarthy took his potshots, attacking the Red menace had become a staple of U.S.

politics. At the turn of the century, the focus had been on radical unionists in the Industrial Workers of the World, or "Wobblies." Before that, it was on "bomb-throwing" German anarchists, who took the fall for all collectivists after the Haymarket Riot (see page 116). The culprits may have varied, but Americans have been consistent in their conviction that a radical redistribution of wealth must not happen here.

The conviction fumed into a passion after the Russian Revolution of 1917. Post–World War I strikes were frequently blamed on hidden Bolsheviks, state legislatures said you couldn't even *talk* about violence as a means of social change, and hundreds of suspected Red aliens—their position on the leftist spectrum didn't matter—were rounded up, put on ships, and deported. During the Big Red Scare of 1919–20, U.S. Attorney General Mitchell Palmer, the "Fighting Quaker," arrested thousands of supposed leftists, deporting hundreds, and boasted grandly that he had stopped a revolution.

In this supercharged atmosphere, a case of robbery that might have passed almost unnoticed became the focus of national—even international—attention. In April 1920, payroll bandits hit a Massachusetts shoe factory, grabbing $15,000 and killing two employees. Witnesses said the holdup men were Italians, and police brought in two who fit the bill: shoemaker Nicola Sacco and fishmonger Bartolomeo Vanzetti. The evidence against the two was no more than circumstantial, but as political scapegoats they were made to order. Not only had they come into the country with the New Immigration (see page 114), but they had also dodged the draft in World War I and were, by their own admission, godless anarchists. They couldn't have been more likely candidates for a railroad job if they had admitted they were allergic to apple pie.

Convicted of murder in the summer of 1921, Sacco and Vanzetti sat in jail for the next six years while liberal sympathizers mounted protests and appeals. If the Red-fearing public was convinced that the two anarchists must have done the crime, the duo's defenders were as confident, and just as illogically so, that public bias meant they must be innocent. Among celebrities who rushed to the Italians' defense were poet Edna St. Vincent Millay, critic H. L. Mencken, and Harvard law professor Felix Frankfurter, who had helped found the American Civil Liberties Union in 1920 and whose brief linked their prosecution to the Red Scare.

When the two were finally sent to the Boston electric chair in 1927, the prison neighborhood was thronged by thousands of sympathetic demonstrators, and five hundred police were on hand to keep order. Their deaths made them instant martyrs not only to fellow anarchists, but to liberals and working people around the world. Although the facts of their case—and their guilt or innocence—are still being debated, they have maintained that lofty position ever since.

TIDBITS: ✪ *Most famous terrorist act committed by an American anarchist: Leon Czolgosz's 1901 assassination of President William McKinley.* ✪ *Most famous Red Scare deportees: "Red Emma" Goldman and her lover, Russian-born revolutionary Alexander Berkman.* ✪ *Other business, 1927: Charles "Lone Eagle" Lindbergh makes the first nonstop solo crossing of the Atlantic, in his monoplane "The Spirit of St. Louis."*

"I Do Not Choose to Run . . ."

Calvin Coolidge, 1928

It is one of the amusing ironies of American history that stern, closemouthed Calvin Coolidge got to preside over the second half of the Roaring Twenties. As Warren G. Harding's vice-president, he had enjoyed esteem by association in the postwar boom, and when Harding died suddenly in 1923, Coolidge not only slipped easily into the White House but managed to distance himself, as the sole white sheep in the family, from the changes of corruption that were laid posthumously at Harding's door. Even the Teapot Dome scandal—in which the administration's interior secretary, Albert Fall, illegally peddled oil leases to wealthy friends—left the Vermont-born Republican free of stain. So his 1924 election was a landslide.

Four more years of limelight, however, proved more than sufficient for him. Although the prosperity brought about (or so the Republicans said) by Coolidge's "don't-rock-business's-boat" attitude would almost certainly have assured him a second full term, he instead chose to retire in quiet Northampton, Massachusetts, whose mayor he had been years before. His announcement to the press was characteristically blunt: "I do not choose to run for president in 1928."

This gem was stylistically in step with previous comments that had earned him the epithet "Silent Cal." Although his biographers paint a Coolidge that was frequently chatty—even voluble on occasion—the laconic persona served him well in public life, and it's this persona that folklore sustains. Here he is on national priorities: "I am for economy. After that I am for more economy." On the value of industrial enterprise: "The business of America is business." On a long-winded sermonizer's view of sin: "He's against it." To a reporter who bet she could get more than two words out of him. "You lose." And to those who felt the United States should allow its wartime allies to renege on their war debts: "They hired the money, didn't they?"

In deciding not to seek reelection, Coolidge showed what might almost be called clairvoyance. He left town in January 1929, handing the reins of government to Herbert Hoover, who had been Harding's—and his own—secretary of commerce.

Nine months later the dam broke, and Hoover was faced with the worst depression in U.S. history.

Black Tuesday
Stock market crash, October 29, 1929

The Great Crash of '29 was caused by a combination of over-production and underconsumption, abetted by a speculative frenzy in the stock market and—not least of all—the rapid, unqualified expansion of installment buying.

What does this mean in English? Well, suppose there's a young couple, Joe and Maisie, who are just starting their lives together. Like most of their peers in the go-go twenties, they are eager to feather their nest with all the creature comforts that the increasingly expansive economy is cranking out—from radios to automobiles to chaise lounges. To pay for them, Joe and Maisie make a down payment—just enough to maintain the seller's confidence. On Wall Street the same thing is going on: speculators are buying "sure things" with 10 percent down payments, and borrowing even that from optimistic bankers.

Eventually, though, Joe and Maisie have to default, managing to keep the radio but giving back the chaise lounge. The chaise lounge manufacturer then cuts back on production.

Other Joes and Maisies, who work for the chaise lounge manufacturer, get laid off. This means they can't buy chaise lounges (or radios) either, and other manufacturers start to get worried. They cut back, more people are laid off, and the bankers get nervous. They start looking not only at Joe and Maisie, but at the high rollers down on Wall Street. Since everybody is over-extended, underpaid, and can't-pay-up, those who lent the money start to tighten the reins. Brokers call in margins. Banks call in loans. But the money that everybody is owed is not really there. It's a vast promissory scheme, with nothing behind it but roaring optimism. On October 29, it falls apart, as speculators unload frantically, trying to escape the very panic their actions are creating.

The outcome wasn't good. In the short run, cheap "penny" stocks evaporated, and even the blue chips turned a ghastly gray: General Electric, for example, was selling for almost $400 a share in September; two weeks after the crash it was at $168. In the same period, Montgomery Ward—purveyor of consumer goods to the millions—went from $138 a share to $49. By Christmas, stockholders had seen approximately $40 billion in certificate value fly rapidly—and for many irretrievably—out the window.

And this was only the beginning. After the Great Crash came the Great Depression. Stock speculators may have made up only a tiny fraction of the U.S. population, but it was an economically critical percentage. Hardest hit on Black Tuesday were the movers and shakers—the people whose investments and factories drove the economy. With them in traction, the entire system wobbled, as economic retrenchment sent "ripple crashes" into millions of homes.

TIDBITS: ✪ *The myth that drove the bull market was sanguinely expressed, just before the crash, by industrialist John Raskob: By putting $15 a month into stocks, he said, a person*

"Brother, Can You Spare a Dime?"

The Great Depression of the 1930s

Conventional wisdom says the Great Depression was caused by the stock market crash of 1929. Many economists dispute this, pointing out that unemployment and industrial retrenchment were both on the rise in the 1920s and were only masked by speculative fortunes in some businesses. The real reasons for the decade-long depression, they say, were that the European economy, never fully recovered from the devastating world war, was further strained by currency devaluations that reduced real wages and by the United States' insistence that the Allies repay their war loans. In an international economy, a weakness anywhere affects the whole, and so here. In the absence of the most common solution for business dips—expansion into new markets—the international economy as a whole suffered, with the United States going down along with everybody else.

The man and woman in the street didn't understand this. What they understood was that they, and their neighbors, were out of work. Between 1929 and 1932, American unemployment figures went from approximately 1.5 million to ten times that— with millions more forced to patch together part-time jobs. Bread lines and soup kitchens became everyday sights, and hundreds of once-skilled workers were reduced to selling pencils, shoestrings, or apples on city streets. At a time when "pulling yourself up by your bootstraps" was a dominant social expectation and "workless" was often translated, unfairly, as "worthless," people began to feel psychological depression as well.

To make the American version of the Great Depression even worse, the early 1930s brought the Midwest a stinging drought. Once-profitable acreage turned into twenty-foot-high sand dunes. Huge dust storms fouled machinery and choked livestock, giving the nation's breadbasket the ominous nickname "Dust Bowl." Foreclosures tripled the amount of land that was worked by tenants rather than, in good old American fashion, owned by the farmers themselves. In Oklahoma, where the drought was worst, whole families piled into jalopies and rattled west to California, where they found, to their dismay, that income possibilities were little better. Some counties lost half their people to this exodus.

Wed to the time-honored but now irrelevant idea of self-reliance, President Herbert Hoover could not ease the misery. He did propose some public-works projects, including the building of Boulder Dam, and he encouraged government loans to banks, businesses, and agricultural organizations. But to most people this meant little. His loan program was widely ridiculed as a "millionaire's dole," and the countless shanty-towns for homeless people that dotted the country were spitefully dubbed "Hoovervilles" in his honor. Not until FDR's New Deal did things begin to look up, and even then it was a long, hard climb.

The unofficial theme song of the decade was the Broadway ditty "Brother, Can You Spare a Dime?" Written by E. Y. Harburg and Jay Gorney, it was first heard by theatergoers in the 1932 musical *Americana* and was quickly picked up as painfully appropriate by millions of others. The "Brother" in the title may or may not have been a political joke, but it certainly had political implications. The U.S. Communist party reached its greatest influence during the Great Depression, and "brother" and "sister" were common forms of address among its members.

TIDBITS: ✪ *The only major power unaffected by the worldwide depression: the isolated, trade-poor Soviet Union.* ✪ *FDR's somber summation of the situation, 1932: "I see one-third of a nation ill fed, ill clothed, ill housed."* ✪ *Best depiction of Okie life: John Steinbeck's novel* The Grapes of Wrath *(1939).*

The Hundred Days
Beginning of the New Deal, 1933

After a campaign in which he promised a "new deal" for the "forgotten man," Franklin Delano Roosevelt became president on March 4, 1933. The confident tone of his administration was set in his inaugural address, when he announced that "the only thing we have to fear is fear itself." To dispel that fear—and to attack the depression that had gripped the country for three years—he set the federal government on the problem like a terrier on a rat, working with Congress to pass a flurry of legislation designed to provide relief, recovery, and reform for the troubled economy.

New Deal solutions were actually put into place on a regular basis until 1939. But the first, phenomenal rush of legislative activity took place during a three-month special session of Congress, from March to June 1933. In that famous "Hundred Days," Congress created the first of the many so-called alphabet agencies by which the New Deal became popularly known. Some highlights:

FDIC. FDR's first extraordinary measure—taken only two days after his inauguration—was to close down the nation's banks. During the five-day bank "holiday" that followed, he got Congress to pass an Emergency Banking Relief Act, which authorized him to regulate banking. Later in the Hundred Days, Congress authorized the Federal Deposit Insurance Corporation, to insure customers' deposits against insolvency.

CCC. Established in March, the Civilian Conservation Corps provided jobs for the urban unemployed in thousands of federal camps around the country. Working for a dollar a day, they planted trees, built dams and bridges, and worked on various other public-works projects. Over the next decade, approximately 2.5 million young men did national service in the CCC.

AAA. To provide relief for embattled farmers—particularly in the Dust Bowl—the Agricultural Adjustment Administration sought to establish a system of price parity by limiting production and thus raising prices. Few farmers saw the logic of "planned scarcity" and were persuaded to oblige only by being paid for not producing.

TVA. A massive public-works program with equally massive environmental implications, the Tennessee Valley Authority put approximately fifteen thousand people to work in the economically hard-hit Tennessee River valley. By cutting channels, constructing locks, and building dams, they established a system that not only prevented flooding but provided the region, for the first time, with reliable electric power.

NIRA. FDR himself called the National Industrial Recovery Act "the most important and far-reaching legislation ever enacted by the American Congress." To mute tensions between labor and business, it set up the National Recovery Administration (NRA) to oversee industry codes regarding pay scales, collective bargaining, child labor, and the like. It also formed the Federal Emergency Relief Administration (FERA), precursor of the better-known Public Works Administration (PWA), which backed projects providing 500,000 jobs.

There was more, but that gives you the idea. By the time the New Deal started to wind down in 1939, Washington's intervention and regulation had created a model for the Big Government we know today, while implementing much of the old Progressive agenda. Among the New Deal innovations that we now take for granted are federal aid to housing, the right to collective bargaining, federal oversight of the stock market, a minimum wage, and social security. And, oh yes, the right to drink in public: FDR's first Congress also knocked down Prohibition.

Unfortunately, the New Deal didn't stamp out the Great Depression. After a remarkable recovery in FDR's first administration, unemployment soared again in the so-called Roosevelt recession of 1937–38, and the stock market didn't get bullish until World War II. But the Democrats' tinkering with the economy provided hope—something Hoover had not been able to do. It also provided jobs, tremendous enthusiasm, tremendous resentment—and, by 1939, a $40 billion deficit. Fifty years ago, that was real money.

TIDBITS: ✪ *Among the more famous employees of the New Deal: photographers Walker Evans and Dorothea Lange, hired by the Farm Security Administration to document the plight of the unemployed.* ✪ *The advisers who helped FDR design the New Deal were known collectively as the "brain trust."*

"Share the Wealth"

Huey Long, 1935

One of the great demagogues of the 1930s was a Louisiana country lawyer who, through his alternatively attractive and repellent populist energy, nearly shook FDR from his throne. Born in 1893, Huey Long first made a name for himself in bayou politics as a public-utilities commissioner, a position he used to assail the rate hikes of major corporations. Between 1921 and 1926 he effectively kept both phone and rail prices down, while waging an animated campaign against the Standard Oil Company. His often successful windmill-tilting made him a darling of the poor, and he became governor in 1928 with the campaign slogan "Every Man a King."

The egalitarianism evident in this pitch was tempered by a thorough devotion to his own aggrandizement. Long used patronage shamelessly, lobbied his legislators with inducements of state jobs, and put many personal expenses on the public tab. On the other hand, he dramatically upgraded Louisiana's highways and public university, provided free schoolbooks for the state's children, and—always and loudly—championed the rights of the "little man" against vested interests.

Because of his appeal to voters, he survived an impeachment attempt and in 1930 was elected to the U.S. Senate. After managing to defer his seating for two years to prevent his lieutenant-governor from succeeding him as governor, he went to Washington in 1932, just as FDR himself was taking office. Originally a strong Roosevelt man, Long soon came to feel that the New York patrician didn't go nearly far enough in attacking the depression. His own solution was a "Share the Wealth" program. Probably the most extensive "transfer payment" operation ever conceived outside of a Communist country, it provided for a $5 million–per-family fortune cap, a top annual income of $1 million, a guaranteed income of about $2,500, and a "homestead allowance" of $6,000 for every family.

Amazingly, at the same time that he was drumming up support for his redistribution scheme, Long was also running his state in absentia, through party stalwarts. From 1934 to 1935, the Baton Rouge state house began, in effect, to legislate municipal government out of existence, giving the D.C.-based Long personal control over the appointment of policemen, firemen, judges, tax assessors, and teachers. The result, in the sobering words of historian David Potter, was "the most complete absolutism that had ever existed in the United States."

Since "the Kingfish," as Long was popularly known, was doing this from two thousand miles away, and since a total redistribution of wealth was not *really* what the New Dealers had in mind, moderates began to feel apprehensive about his plans. Consequently, when Long announced in the summer of 1935 that he might run against FDR that November, the president's supporters went on red alert, warning the electorate that if Long were voted in, the entire country would become his private fief.

As it happened, the voters never got a chance to decide. On September 8, surrounded by bodyguards, Long was fatally shot in the Baton Rouge capitol he had ruled for so long. Two days later he was dead, and with him went the "Share the Wealth" dream. He left behind a reputation for amplified vision and scurrilous conduct that is unsurpassed in American history. Nationally he is thought of as a loudmouth upstart, but in Louisiana his reputation is better, especially among old folks who remember his twisted populism as a lost ideal.

TIDBITS: ✪ *Political family ties: Huey's wife served out his term in the Senate, a brother and son also went to Congress, and another brother, Earl, was thrice elected governor of the Bayou State.* ✪ *His literary legacy:* Every Man a King *(1933) and the happily anticipatory* My First Days in the White House *(1935).*

"Nine Old Men"

"Packing" the Court, 1937

Not everybody loved the New Deal. To conservatives, such massive tinkering with the economy was nothing more or less than "creeping socialism." They widely reviled its architect as Franklin Deficit Roosevelt, as "Rooseveltski," and, with scathing anonymity, as "that man in the White House." Factory owners who thought nothing of cutting production to stimulate prices gasped when the federal government did the same through the AAA's price-parity program. Many Republicans said government handouts discouraged honest labor, and that the New Deal, at best, was wasteful. At worst, it was destroying the system it was trying to save. Left alone, the economy would right itself through "market forces."

Among those who sympathized with this laissez-faire view were a slim majority of the nine Supreme Court justices. Beginning in 1935, the Court began to invalidate some New Deal legislation on constitutional grounds. First to go was Roosevelt's "important and far-reaching" NIRA (see page 162), which the justices saw as giving unwarranted authority to the president. Next was a railroad workers' retirement act, a farm bankruptcy act, a minimum wage law, and the entire Agricultural

Adjustment Administration, which was knocked down because it paid for farming subsidies from an unconstitutional tax on food processors. By the 1936 election, judicial dismantling of the New Deal was under way.

In that election, FDR defeated Republican Alf Landon by the largest electoral margin in U.S. history (523 to 8). Taking the victory as a mandate for his programs, he went to Congress with a highly unusual suggestion designed to bring the "Nine Old Men," as he contemptuously called them, in line with the rest of the country. To get some new blood into the Court, he asked the legislature to give him the power to appoint one extra Supreme Court justice for every one of them over the age of seventy who would not retire—with an upper limit on the bench of fifteen.

Loyal New Dealers viewed this Judiciary Reorganization Bill as court "reform," but FDR's critics, who knew Caesarism when they smelled it, called it "court-packing," and it was they who prevailed: the bill was killed by the Senate in committee. FDR, however, had made his point—so effectively that the Court's sentiments began to shift. In subsequent decisions they warmed up to the New Deal, approving among other measures a women's minimum wage, the National Labor Relations Act (which empowered workers to form collective-bargaining unions), and social security. Deaths of and resignations by the justices opened the way to further liberalization, and by the time of his death FDR had appointed nine justices—more than any other president in U.S. history.

Court-packing may have been a ridiculous idea, but it did not, as is often supposed, subvert the Constitution. That document provides for a Supreme Court and gives the president power to appoint its justices. It says nothing about how many may be appointed. Originally the high court had six justices. The number went up and down during the nineteenth century and only settled at the current number of nine in 1869.

"Arsenal of Democracy"

Franklin D. Roosevelt, 1940

As European fascism and Japanese imperialism jointly threatened international security throughout the late 1930s, most Americans wanted to avoid involvement. There was no affection for Hitler, Tojo, or Mussolini, but there was also, for the most part, an unwillingness on the American side to fight such territorial and political advances. Traditional isolationism factored into the Americans' reluctance. So did resentment over Europe's lingering war debt and frustration with a still-depressed economy. The common feeling was that tyranny's victims should help themselves; the United States had enough problems right at home.

As early as 1934, isolationist pressure had led to passage of the Johnson Debt Default Act, which prohibited private loans to debtor nations then in arrears. That same year, a Senate committee began to investigate charges that U.S. munitions manufacturers had engaged in wartime profiteering. When the big surprise came that they had, isolationism received a major boost, and between 1935 and 1939, Neutrality Acts banned U.S. shipments to warring nations as well as the arming of merchant vessels. Tragically, these supposedly defensive gestures came in response to such dress rehearsals for World War II as Italy's invasion of Ethiopia (1935) and the Spanish civil war (1936–39).

Chief among the opponents of this ostrichlike legislation was President Franklin D. Roosevelt, whose requests for naval appropriations in his second term got him branded by the isolationist consensus as a warmonger. After the Ethiopian incursion and Japan's 1937 invasion of China, he made a stirring call to embargo, or "quarantine," such aggressors. Isolationist sentiment, however, continued to hold. It was 1938 before FDR got his naval monies, and a year after that before the Neutrality Acts were loosened up to permit "cash and carry" shipments to France and England. Conveniently, this revised policy also stimulated U.S. industries, which is what finally solved the troubled decade's unemployment problem.

The final step in the nation's shift toward involvement came only months before the attack on Pearl Harbor. Late in 1940, just after beating Wendell Wilkie for an unprecedented third term, FDR circumvented the war-debt objection by suggesting we *lend*—rather than sell—the Allies arms. America then would become, in his famous phrase, the "arsenal of democracy," and once Nazism was beaten back, the Allies could give the arms back to us. Congress approved the idea the following March, with an initial outlay of $7 billion to cover the costs of the so-called Lend-Lease program.

Not surprisingly, the German führer was less than pleased. Although the "arsenal of democracy" had not officially declared war on Germany, it didn't have to. Shipping arms to the Allies, on whatever terms, put the United States in the same position that she had been in twenty-five years earlier, as a "neutral" supplier on the eve of World War I. Similar conditions, similar result. German U-boats once again went on the attack, and American vessels once again became the targets. When the U.S. destroyer *Reuben James* was sunk off Iceland that October, American noninvolvement went to the bottom with its crew.

Two weeks later, Congress voted to arm merchantmen, and the American people prepared their minds for another war.

"A Date Which Will Live in Infamy"

Franklin D. Roosevelt, December 8, 1941

The date in question? The previous day: Sunday, December 7, when at eight o'clock in the morning, Honolulu time, Japanese planes swept out of the sky to inflict massive casualties on the U.S. fleet at Pearl Harbor. This surprise attack was, of course, the beginning of active American involvement in World War II. When President Roosevelt learned what had happened, he prepared a message to Congress that began with the "infamy" line and ended with a request to go to war. A half hour later, Congress obliged, and the United States joined France and Britain against the Berlin-Rome-Tokyo Axis.

That America should have been pulled finally into the conflict was not surprising. By 1941, not only were we arming the Allies as the "arsenal of democracy," but in the Atlantic Charter, issued that August, President Roosevelt and Britain's Winston Churchill had announced their common devotion to Allied war aims. So some sort of attack should have been expected. But its direction, as it happened, was unanticipated. Most experts thought the real threat lay in the North Atlantic, where American destroyers had already been deployed and where two had been sunk by German U-boats.

Nobody was in doubt about Japan's imperial ambitions, and in fact we had already reacted to them by freezing her assets. But in 1941 Japan's ambitions were focused on Southeast Asia, especially the oil-rich Netherlands East Indies. The American forces that seemed truly threatened by Japan were in the nearby Philippines, under Douglas MacArthur. No one took very seriously the idea that the Rising Sun might decide to attack Hawaii.

Historians still debate why this miscalculation was so endemic, but endemic it was. Some observers said that, as ill prepared for war as the United States was at the time, the Pacific Fleet was still a sufficient deterrent to inhibit the Japanese from opening a two-front offensive; when they moved, it would be to their south, and it was there they'd dig in. Others said that precisely because our nation was not ready to fight— isolationist sentiment was still strong—the Japanese would not perceive Pearl Harbor as a threat and would leave it, conveniently, alone. Whether through smugness or excessive humility, though, it's clear that FDR's people dropped the ball. The Pacific Fleet commander, Admiral Husband Kimmel, proclaimed in November that there was "no probability" of an attack on his command, while U.S. intelligence, after it had broken the Japanese code, neglected to keep Kimmel apprised of its diplomatic negotiations, or even to send Pearl Harbor a decoding machine. Had the admiral been made aware a little earlier that our negotiations had broken down on December 6—and thus that an attack was imminent—Sunday's carnage might have been lessened.

As it happened, the carnage was considerable. U.S. carriers were on sea maneuvers—an enormous stroke of luck, since they turned the tide in the Pacific two years later—but the battle-ships and fighter planes were devastated. Only one of eight battle wagons escaped unharmed, and more than half of our four hundred planes were damaged or destroyed. More than twenty-four hundred service people lost their lives, and well over another thousand were wounded. No wonder "Remember Pearl Harbor" became the Pacific's principal battle cry.

In the inevitable parceling-out of blame, Kimmel got the brunt of the criticism and was relieved of his command within a month (later inquiries cleared his reputation). FDR also took the rap. His more conspiratorially minded foes went so far as to hint that FDR had invited the attack as a way of getting us sideways into the war. The president's longtime friend and biographer Joseph Alsop has called such suggestions "vile," but they were taken seriously enough at the time.

TIDBITS: ✪ *The Japanese code message indicating that the attack had been successful: "Tora! Tora! Tora!" Literal transla-tion: "Tiger! Tiger! Tiger!"* ✪ *"Infamy" was a revision on the president's part. FDR's original draft read "a date which will live in world history."* ✪ *The most seriously hit battleship, the* Arizona, *went down with more than a thousand men on board. The site of its shattered hull is now a national monument.*

Truman Doctrine

Harry Truman, 1947

A political priority after all wars is to restore the economic health of the combatants. After World War II that priority took on special meaning for the United States, which saw that in addition to being incapacitated as a trading partner, Europe was now vulnerable to a new threat: the postwar opportunism of Stalin's Russia. To prevent the westward advance of what Winston Churchill had called the Iron Curtain, President Truman in March 1947 proclaimed a policy with far more radical implications than its predecessor the Monroe Doctrine (see page 57). According to the Truman Doctrine, the United States would henceforth be committed to the containment of Communist expansion, not just in "our" hemisphere, but in Europe as well.

To put this new policy into operation, Truman asked Congress for an initial outlay of $400 million in aid for Communist-infiltrated Greece and Turkey. This request was seconded, in a more elaborate declaration, three months later at Harvard University. The principal speaker at the Crimson commencement exercises that June was Secretary of State George C. Marshall, who during the war had been army chief of staff. Convinced that infusions of American aid were the only protection against Stalin's schemes, Marshall proposed "substantial additional help" to Europe as a way of avoiding "economic, social, and political deterioration of very grave character." To mute Soviet objections to the plan, he included East Bloc countries as aid recipients. Russia went so far as to attend the first planning conference but soon backed out—along with her allies—and the Marshall Plan, as it came to be called, thenceforth applied only to the West.

The first concrete implementation of the Truman Doctrine, the Marshall Plan was a huge success. Between 1948 and 1952, through the Economic Cooperation Administration (ECA), U.S. taxpayers sent more than $13 billion to Europe in the form of direct grants, food, consumer goods, and tariff reductions; these were administered in Europe by a recipient agency, the Organization for European Economic Cooperation (OEEC). On average, the Europeans' GNP went up 25 percent in this period, and industrial production shot up by one-third. By the time Truman left office, Western Europe was still wobbly, but upright, and the political aim of the program—containment of Communism—had been reasonably well realized. Red partisans in the Greek mountains were defeated, and France and Italy would not have strong Communist movements again for almost twenty years.

The Marshall Plan was the acute phase of the Truman Doctrine. The Doctrine's more enduring feature was the North Atlantic Treaty Organization (NATO), founded in 1949. A military alliance of Western European nations, the United States, and Canada, it provided the principal bulwark for a generation against the continued fear of Soviet expansion, and was—along with the Soviets' counterpart, the Warsaw pact—one of the two major player groups of the cold war. Up through the 1980s conservative Americans viewed the survival of NATO as tantamount to survival itself.

Marshall, who had first seen service in the Philippines during its 1902 insurrection, distinguished himself in World War I before becoming army head in 1939. Churchill called him the "true organizer of victory" since he had directed the planning of the Normandy invasion. Active after the war in developing NATO and lobbying for better military training, he also won the Nobel Peace Prize in 1953—the only professional soldier ever to do so.

TIDBITS: ✪ *The third arm of Truman's containment trident: the 1950 Point Four program, which called for technical aid to underdeveloped countries.* ✪ *Biggest aid package under the Marshall Plan: $3.1 billion to Great Britain. Smallest package: $32 million to Iceland.* ✪ *Most famous OEEC progeny: today's European Common Market.*

Cold War

Postwar Soviet-American tensions

The cold war was never all that cold. The phrase itself—popularized by political columnist Walter Lippman—was a hopeful euphemism for "non-total war"; it promised that in the wake of World War II, the conflict between "godless Communism" and the "free world" would proceed regionally and sporadically rather than all at once. Better than Armageddon, although little comfort to the dead of Korea and Vietnam.

The two Asian engagements were the most protracted cold war campaigns, although certainly not the only ones. Between 1945, when the Soviets and the West started jockeying for position in Europe, and 1990, when the Berlin Wall came tumbling down, the planet hosted hundreds of regional explosions which, within their own small circumferences, were just as hot as Monte Cassino or Guadalcanal. The two Great Powers fed these fires, battling to bring this or that peasant economy into accord with the Pentagon's or the Kremlin's designs.

It wasn't all a matter of shooting, of course. A lot of it was getting ready for shooting, or developing nuclear capabilities which, according to the period's deterrence theory, were supposed to keep the Big Shoot—nuclear annihilation—from occurring. Throughout most of the cold war period, the threat of the atomic bomb was a primary spur to action, and bomb secrets were the greater part of keeping score. The CIA and the KGB, when they weren't destabilizing foreign governments, sweated mightily to keep secrets out of each other's hands, and the most celebrated civilian casualties of the long conflict, Ethel and Julius Rosenberg, were executed in 1953 for nuclear espionage.

Their deaths, fiercely protested by liberals, were one indication of the anti-Communist fever that gripped America throughout the period. Another was the brief but rabid reign of Joseph McCarthy (see page 182), the junior senator from Wisconsin who terrorized dozens of people into fingering "Commie sympathizers" until he was finally censured by his peers in 1954. Among "Tail-gunner Joe's" contributions to history was the encouragement of such phrases as "pinko," "soft on Communism," and "guilt by association."

People still talk about the McCarthy "witch hunts," although they commonly forget what the hunting was about. Partisans disagree on that even now, but basically the explanations for the cold war break down as follows:

1. The American argument: The cold war was about protecting Western democracy from totalitarian tyrants. (We're talking about democrats like Cuba's Fulgencio Batista and tyrants like Chile's Salvador Allende.)

2. The Soviet (and later Chinese) argument: It was about protecting socialist democracy from capitalist tyrants. (Here we focus on democrats like Fidel Castro and tyrants like Czechoslovakia's Alexander Dubcek.)

3. The argument of blunt Marxists and one or two disingenuous capitalists: It was about who should control tractor sales to Ruritania—that is, whether American capitalism or international socialism should govern the distribution of goods and services to a hungry planet.

4. The psychosocial explanation: It was about Red boys and red-white-and-blue boys in the sandbox—grabbing toys, throwing sand, that sort of thing.

Historians differ not only on the ultimate "reasons" for the tension, but also on its duration. The first fifteen years are clear enough (see *Tidbits*, below), but after that it gets fuzzily partisan. Was the 1965 American invasion of the Dominican Republic part of the cold war? How about the Soviet Union's crushing of the 1968 Prague spring? The U.S. in Cambodia? The U.S.S.R. in Afghanistan? Cuba in Angola? Ronald Reagan in Grenada? And so on.

There's some debate over whether the cold war has ended, even now. Rigid constructionists give a death date of 1963, when—two years after the Cuban missile crisis—the U.S. and the U.S.S.R. signed the first nuclear test-ban treaty. Middle-of-the-roaders throw out 1972, when the Strategic Arms Limitation Treaty (SALT) talks got under way and when cold warrior *numero uno* himself, Richard Nixon, paid visits to both Moscow and Peking. Others favor a more recent date: say the demuralization of Berlin, 1990, or the Gorbachev-Bush talks of the same year. There are even those who say the thing won't really be over until the CIA and KGB either merge or disband.

TIDBITS: ✪ *Cold war chronology at a glance: 1947 Truman Doctrine defines the American policy of "containment"; 1949 Germany divides into capitalist West Germany and socialist East Germany; North Atlantic Treaty Organization (NATO) established to provide mutual support against Communist expansion; China falls to Mao Zedong's Communist rebels; 1948–49 Soviets blockade West Berlin; United States responds by airlifting in supplies; 1950–53 Korean conflict; 1956 Hungarian revolution crushed by Soviet tanks; 1959 Cuban revolution brings Fidel Castro to power; 1961 Cuban missile crisis keeps Soviet missiles out of Cuba. ✪ Most famous cold war draftee: Elvis Presley, posted to Germany (1958–60).*

"Old Soldiers Never Die. They Just Fade Away."

Douglas MacArthur, 1951

With the exception of George Armstrong Custer, Douglas MacArthur was probably the most colorfully theatrical self-promoter in U.S. Army history. And when it came to their most salient mutual characteristic—arrogance—MacArthur may have outdone even the boy general. Custer contented himself with flouting the orders of West Point superiors and field commanders, but MacArthur went straight to the top: He bucked the authority of three U.S. presidents.

His first brush was with Herbert Hoover, president in the first years of the Great Depression. In that sorry time, among those clamoring for public relief were a ragtag "army" of World War I veterans who, in May 1932, converged on Washington to demand an early release of their military bonuses. After being turned down by Congress, most of this Bonus Army left town. But a couple of thousand, still camped in shantytowns in July, became such an embarrassment to Hoover that he sent MacArthur, then army chief of staff, to clear them out. MacArthur, himself a World War I vet, blithely ignored the president's order to act gradually and with minimum force; instead, he tear-gassed his former buddies and burned their shacks, becoming Hoover's biggest embarrassment of that year.

MacArthur's second run-in came with Franklin D. Roosevelt. In 1942, when MacArthur, as the Pacific theater's supreme Allied commander, was driven from the Philippines by Japanese troops, he vowed in a famous parting shot, "I shall return." Two years later, when the Japanese were retreating westward, FDR ordered him to bypass the Philippines and drive them directly toward Tokyo. MacArthur objected strongly, and FDR relented, allowing the general to wade ashore at the Philippines' Leyte Gulf for the cameras. A year later, MacArthur was able to accept the Japanese surrender in Tokyo Bay.

A third run-in, which was more obviously an example of insubordination, got MacArthur relieved of his command. The year was 1951, the war was the Korean "police action," and the commander in chief was Harry Truman. MacArthur, then seventy years old and in command of U.N. forces, had pushed the invading North Koreans almost to the Chinese border when Truman, fearing a third world war, called a stop. MacArthur persisted, thus inciting the Chinese to send 200,000 men to the aid of their North Korean fellow Communists. The president then said again to hold on. MacArthur's idea of holding on was to refrain from invading China itself, although he did—publicly and loudly—recommend bombing and blockading the country. While Truman attempted to negotiate a peace, MacArthur continued to ignore his orders and ridicule his policy until, on April 11, Truman "invited" him home.

With the anti-Red fervor of the time, and the congenital American affection for maverick warriors, the general was lionized even more for being fired than he had been for his intemperate saber-rattling. In a speech given to Congress upon his return, he made it clear that he had been emboldened rather than chastened by his experience when he laid out, once again, his hard-line stance. The "old soldiers" quote with which he ended the address—taken from a barracks ballad—lent him a specious aura of humility, and it has brought lumps to throats for forty years. Nearly forgotten is Truman's explanation for his action: "General MacArthur is one of our greatest military commanders. But the cause of world peace is more important than any individual."

TIDBITS: ✪ *MacArthur's aspirations for the GOP nomination in 1952 were thwarted when his former aide, Dwight D. Eisenhower, got the nod.* ✪ *One replay of MacArthur's gung-ho policy was General Curtis LeMay's advice during the Vietnam War: "Bomb them back into the Stone Age."* ✪ *Hero trademarks: Custer had long hair and red scarves; MacArthur had a corncob pipe and aviator shades.*

"The Silent Generation"

1950s catchphrase

This misnomer was heard occasionally in the fifties, but it came into its own in the troubled sixties, referring retroactively to the supposed dull complacency of the flower children's parents. The sixties were of course a noisy decade, and according to its young participants also a visionary one. According to the given wisdom of the time, the previous decade had been both mute and blind. The so-called Silent Generation's bourgeois ideal had been to settle down, slave for corporate America, move to the suburbs, put a Chevy in the garage and a barbecue pit in the yard, and raise 2.3 perfect children to the strains of the "I Love Lucy" theme.

That this "Leave It to Beaver" stereotype bore *some* relation to reality is clear enough. Marriage and family did become postwar ideals, with the resulting "baby boom" becoming the era's demographic keynote. In a rapidly expanding economy replete with new home conveniences, consumer purchasing did rise dramatically, with citizens showing a marked fondness for flashy cars and "dream kitchens." People did move to the suburbs, and plenty of them put in barbecue pits. And there was a rise in "corporatism" as a way of life, as returning servicemen shed their khaki for gray flannel and settled in to the humdrum business of techno-management. Sociologist William Whyte was not far off the mark when he identified the "organization man" as a workplace ideal.

But if you suppose this was all there was to the fifties, then (as my grandfather used to say), "You wasn't there, Charlie." The allegedly boring postwar period also saw crippling strikes by miners and steelworkers, a growing antagonism between Big Business and Big Labor, congressional investigations into organized crime, an explosion of juvenile delinquency, the Korean War, the civil-rights movement, antibomb rallies, "beatniks," "folkniks," and, oh yes, rock 'n' roll. The fifties were about as silent as a roller coaster.

As for the decade's parental "generation"—the Ward and June Cleaver types who had sold their souls for material comforts—it's nonsense to suppose they shared a common vision. Plenty of them wanted only security—an unsurprising ideal for folks who had weathered the worst depression and the worst war in world history—but there were many who had other purposes in mind. Among the members of the Silent Generation, for example, were such people as folk singer Pete Seeger (born 1917), social critics John Kenneth Galbraith (1908) and C. Wright Mills (1916), bohemian authors Allen Ginsberg (1926) and Jack Kerouac (1922), and feminist pioneer Betty Friedan (1921). Speaking of the fifties as a Silent Generation is like saying Victorian England had no Oscar Wilde or Jack the Ripper.

TIDBITS: ✪ *The birthrate explosion after World War II, commonly called the baby boom, meant 28 million new Americans in the 1950s.* ✪ *The great triad of "perfect families" in TV's Golden Age: the Nelsons ("Ozzie and Harriet," 1952–66), the Cleavers ("Leave It to Beaver," 1957–63), and the Andersons ("Father Knows Best," 1954–62).* ✪ *Medical breakthrough of the decade: Jonas Salk's polio vaccine (1954).* ✪ *Song of the decade: "Blue Suede Shoes" (1956).*

"205 Card-carrying Communists"

Senator Joseph McCarthy, 1950

The late 1940s was a period that increasingly saw the spread of Communism. By 1947, Eastern Europe was becoming so Sovietized that President Truman, in his eponymous doctrine, had to announce a "containment" policy. The following year China fell to Communist rebel Mao Zedong, and the year after that, Russia got the bomb. American conservatives, feeling threatened on all sides, looked for someone to take the blame. They found plenty of candidates right at home—many of them, evidently, working for the government.

On the Hill, both houses of Congress went after citizens who were thought to have secret ties to Stalin's Kremlin. In the House, the investigating body was the zealous HUAC, or House Un-American Activities Committee. Formed a decade earlier to uncover Nazi propagandists, it turned its attention after the war to "pinko" influences and soon ferreted out scores of "subversives." The most famous one was probably Alger Hiss, a State Department official who, in 1948, was accused of espionage; his later conviction for perjury helped make the reputation of young congressman and HUAC member Richard Nixon.

Other celebrated HUAC targets were the moviemakers who became known as the Hollywood Ten. Accused in 1947 of Communist affiliations, they refused to give evidence to the committee or to finger anyone else. This got them characterized as "unfriendly witnesses" and then blacklisted. For more than a decade, with the compliance of studio heads, such writers as Ring Lardner, Jr., and Dalton Trumbo were officially banned from working in their industry.

Fervent as HUAC was, though, anti-Communist "witch

hunting" was to reach its peak in the 1950s, with the bizarre posturing of Senator Joseph McCarthy. Historian Frederick Siegel calls him, in a wonderful phrase, the "tribune of revenge." At the time, McCarthy had a host of other epithets. Most commonly he was "the junior senator from Wisconsin." Because he had claimed aerial combat experience in World War II, he was known as "Tail-gunner Joe." And, because he supported the soft-drink industry's attempts to decontrol sugar prices, he was also called the "Pepsi Cola Kid."

None of these names gives an adequate sense of how gravely sobering McCarthy, and the McCarthy period, were. "McCarthyism" is, for many liberals, still shorthand for conservative attacks on freedom of expression, and although it's unfair to lay all intolerance at McCarthy's door, there's no question that he was intolerant. Not to mention brash, theatrical, utterly contemptuous of facts—and extremely powerful.

His Red-baiting career began in 1950, when during a speech in West Virginia he waved a paper in the air, claiming it contained the names of "205 card-carrying Communists" then on the payroll of the U.S. State Department. He never revealed the names, and congressional hearings later found the charge baseless. Ironically, though, the hearings also made his reputation, especially among Republicans, who felt that Truman—author of the containment policy—was "soft on Communism." Three years after his initial sally, McCarthy became chair of the Senate Committee on Government Operations. In this post he became the conservatives' media star, finding Communist influence at all levels of Eisenhower's government.

For liberal America, the real problem was at the grass-roots level. As unsubstantiated as McCarthy's charges proved to be, they fed a widespread fear that the nation was being undermined by Moscow's lackeys. In hundreds of towns, the Tail-gunner's tactics were replicated on a smaller scale. Library shelves were cleansed of "socialist" texts like *Robin Hood*, the proposed fluoridation of municipal water supplies was voted down as a Commie trick, and countless people lost their jobs on mere suspicion.

The junior senator rode high until 1954, when he made the fatal error, on national television, of attacking the U.S. Army. After making little headway in identifying military subversion, he accused army counsel Joseph N. Welch of having on his staff a young subversive lawyer. Welch's tear-filled repudiation of McCarthy's "recklessness" put a human spin on the senator's crusade, and the hearings ended with McCarthy's fall from public grace. Six months later, when his fellow senators officially condemned his "contemptuous, contumacious, and denunciatory" behavior, Joe McCarthy began to fade from public life. The term "McCarthyism" remains, however, as does his secure place in liberal demonology.

TIDBITS: ✪ *Dalton Trumbo, blacklisted from 1947 until 1960, wrote the Oscar-winning screenplay for* The Brave One *(1956) under the pseudonym Robert Rich.* ✪ *Best HUAC memoir: Lillian Hellman's* Scoundrel Time *(1976).* ✪ *Most famous McCarthy targets: Eisenhower's secretaries of state and defense, Dean Acheson and George C. Marshall, respectively, whose anti-Communist stances McCarthy saw as too "soft."*

"Military-Industrial Complex"

Dwight D. Eisenhower, 1961

"Beware of the military-industrial complex" sounds like the warning of a Vietnam War peacenik or a Reagan-era Democrat lamenting the substitution of bombers for social programs.

Certainly antimilitarists have condemned the "complex" repeatedly, but the first person actually to use the phrase was a four-star general who had engineered the greatest military victory in world history—the Allied defeat of Nazi Germany.

The occasion was a televised farewell address delivered just days before JFK took over the reins of government. In it outgoing President Eisenhower warned that a recently developed "conjunction" of "an immense military establishment and a large arms industry" boded ill for the American system, in a political, economic, and even "spiritual" sense. "In the councils of government," he said, "we must guard against the acquisition of unwarranted influence, whether sought or unsought, by the military-industrial complex. The potential for the disastrous rise of misplaced power exists and will persist."

No one should read this prescient warning as evidence that Ike was soft on the issue of defense. The former World War II European supreme commander recognized clearly the importance of a strong military. It was on his watch that the cold war really began to heat up, and Ike was not above sending American troops to the Middle East and Southeast Asia to contain Communism. What he objected to was not defense spending per se, but its wasteful and self-aggrandizing nature. Well before Senator William Proxmire started giving Golden Fleece awards to Pentagon contractors for padding their bills, Eisenhower was identifying the hazards of our purchasing policy, ridiculing the ways in which, to quote his biographer Elmo Richardson, "industrial lobbies tended to protect existing or potential investments when contracting for production of supplies and weapons." What Ike hated was the old-boy defense network, in which military efficiency took a back seat to corporate gain.

We know all about that now, of course, what with revelations of the Pentagon paying $150 for a hammer and three times that for a toilet seat. But in Ike's day such things were not widely known, and he should be credited for bringing the potential for abuse, as well as the catchphrase, into public discourse. In addition, we may thank him for a solution. What he proposed, as a basic defense posture, was not mere expansion, but more bang for the buck—specifically, a trimming of troop numbers and a greater reliance on sophisticated technology to help this leaner, meaner force function better.

T I D B I T S : ✪ *Ike's most far-reaching military decision: establishment of the 1957 Eisenhower Doctrine, which asserted the U.S. right to use force against "international Communism" in the Middle East.* ✪ *Author of the phrase "military-industrial complex": Eisenhower speechwriter Malcolm Moos.*

"Ask Not What Your Country Can Do for You . . ."

John F. Kennedy, 1961

When Massachusetts senator John Fitzgerald Kennedy defeated Richard Nixon for the presidency in 1960, he became not only the youngest man ever elected to the office, but far and away the most stylish. With his winning smile, classy verve, and easy wit, he overcame encumbrances that might have buried a lesser man. He was a Catholic, but because he didn't seem terribly serious about it, even the paranoid believed the Pope might not be a threat. His family made most other wealthy families look like the Beverly Hillbillies, but JFK had a common touch about him that offset this social stigma. And even though he'd attended Harvard and written books, no one thought of him as an egghead. All in all, with his charming wife, the former

Jacqueline Bouvier, and cute Bostonian accent, JFK was a breath of fresh air.

He set an unmistakable tone for his administration at the outset, announcing during the campaign that he wanted to lead Americans toward a "New Frontier" and challenging them in his inaugural address to put national goals above partisan and personal aims. "Ask not what your country can do for you," he said. "Ask what you can do for your country." Millions of Americans took this challenge to heart and believed that, with the young man from "Bahston," anything was possible.

In reality the New Frontier didn't stretch very far, at least on the domestic front. Among the items on the young president's wish list were a higher minimum wage, more public housing, Medicare for the elderly, civil-rights legislation, and federal help for education. He didn't live to see any of this happen, although his successor, the far more skillful arm-twister Lyndon Johnson, incorporated many of these aims into his Great Society agenda (see page 193).

Internationally JFK's policies fared a little better. Good cold warrior that he was, he tried overall to keep the Reds in geopolitical check. In Southeast Asia, this meant increasing U.S. support of the anti-Communist Diem regime from several hundred to several thousand "advisers." In Europe it meant confronting a swaggering Nikita Khrushchev—who responded to the confrontation with the Berlin Wall. Closer to home it meant fretting over Fidel Castro, who had established a Communist presence, as they said at the time, "ninety miles from Miami Beach." That presence led Kennedy in 1961 to back the ill-fated Bay of Pigs invasion, in which Cuban counter-revolutionaries were badly beaten by Castro forces. It also generated the following year's fearful Missile Crisis, in which a U.S. naval blockade intended to keep Russian missiles out of the Caribbean island brought the United States and the Soviet Union to the brink of war.

On a less belligerent note, Kennedy's foreign policy also

included the Alliance for Progress, an aid program to discourage Communism in Latin America; a 1963 nuclear test-ban treaty with the Russians; and his most endearing—and enduring—legacy, the Peace Corps. Founded in 1961 under State Department auspices, the organization was designed officially "to help foreign countries meet their urgent needs for skilled manpower," but its political agenda was also obvious to all but the blind. Peace Corps volunteers have always served the double purpose of providing assistance while enlisting support for the American way. More than any other group of New Frontiersmen, the Corps' young people embodied the ideals of Kennedy's inaugural plea.

Kennedy was killed by gunfire in Dallas on November 22, 1963. The government's investigation, made public in the Warren Report, concluded that a single sniper, Lee Harvey Oswald, was responsible. More elaborate conspiracy theories, indicting everyone from Fidel Castro to the mafia to Lyndon B. Johnson, have surfaced throughout the years, but since Oswald himself was murdered two days after the assassination, it is unlikely that the truth will ever be known.

Although his vice-president, LBJ, made many of Kennedy's domestic dreams a reality, it's not hyperbole to say that with the young Bostonian was buried the innocence of a generation. Posthumous revelations of his womanizing and lack of aggressiveness on civil rights have done little to tarnish his image as a last, best hope. The American public nostalgically views the tenure of Jack and wife Jackie as—to use the 1960s term—an American "Camelot."

TIDBITS: ✪ *Nepotism, Kennedy style: JFK's brother Robert became his attorney general, while his brother-in-law Sargent Shriver became director of the Peace Corps.* ✪ *JFK's collection of biographies,* Profiles in Courage, *won a 1957 Pulitzer Prize.*

> ✪ *JFK's famous announcement at the Berlin Wall, "Ich bin ein Berliner," was supposed to mean "I am a Berliner." What it actually means is "I am a jelly doughnut."*

"I Have a Dream . . ."
Martin Luther King, 1963

The civil-rights movement that has been called the "second Negro emancipation" began symbolically on May 17, 1954, when the Supreme Court handed down a momentous decision in the case of *Brown v. Board of Education*. In striking down a Topeka, Kansas, educational directive that black and white children attend separate schools, the Court reversed the "separate but equal" doctrine that had been established by the *Plessy v. Ferguson* decision of 1896, giving civil-rights activists the thin wedge they had been working for to put an end to nationwide segregation. Before 1954, such organizations as the National Association for the Advancement of Colored People (1910) and the Congress of Racial Equality (1942) had fought discrimination in a legal vacuum. After *Brown*, they had the Constitution on their side.

As might be expected, concrete attempts to put the new ruling into effect were not welcomed in the land of Jim Crow (see page 110). In 1957, when nine black teenagers attempted to register at a Little Rock, Arkansas, white high school, they faced jeers, thrown bottles, and the state's governor, Orville Faubus, who cited "states' rights" as he physically blocked their entry into the school. A similar welcome greeted James Meredith in 1962, when he enrolled at the University of Mississippi.

In both cases, federal troops had to be sent in to ensure local compliance with the Constitution.

But educational institutions were not the only bastions of segregation to be attacked. One year after the *Brown* decision, a young minister named Martin Luther King, Jr., organized a boycott of the Montgomery, Alabama, bus lines which, after a year and several racist bombings, led to their integration. Similar boycotts sprang up throughout the South, as did other, more provocative, forms of activism. Beginning in 1960, at public lunch counters in many states, black and white activists staged patient "sit-ins," requesting service in violation of the businesses' custom of separate counters. In the summer of 1961, under CORE auspices, hundreds of young people, both black and white, integrated buses on so-called Freedom Rides, designed to challenge the separate-but-equal seating arrangements in public transportation. Despite the movement's insistently nonviolent character, more than four hundred Freedom Riders were jailed, many were beaten, and at least three were killed.

Emerging from this ferment as an eloquent leader, and the chief architect of the nonviolent strategy, was Dr. Martin Luther King, Jr. After the bus boycott, he turned his attention to registering black voters and organizing mass protest marches. In August 1963, singing the movement's unofficial anthem, "We Shall Overcome," a quarter of a million people converged on the Lincoln Memorial to hear King deliver the rhetorical masterpiece of his career, his stirring "I have a dream" oration. The dream? Integration, of course, but King portrayed it in tones of such ringing passion that many equated it with the Earthly Paradise. When he dreamed aloud that his children, along with "all God's children," would one day be judged by the "content of their character" rather then the color of their skin, he challenged the nation as it had never been so brilliantly challenged before to fulfill the promise of its own Declaration.

The following year, on paper, the promise was fulfilled with the passage of the 1964 Civil Rights Act. This act, along with the 1965 Voting Rights Act, opened the way for something that hadn't been seen since Reconstruction: the election of black school-board members, black mayors, black legislators. This didn't ensure equality or justice—as the Black Panthers would point out a few years later—but it was a long way from *Plessy v. Ferguson*.

TIDBITS : ✪ *Plaintiff in the 1954 case: eleven-year-old Topeka schoolgirl Linda Brown.* ✪ *First move toward the Montgomery boycott: the refusal of NAACP official Rosa Parks to move to the back of a segregated bus.* ✪ *Reacting to Klan violence during the Freedom Ride summer, Attorney General Robert Kennedy suggested a "cooling off" period to CORE leader James Farmer. Farmer's reply: "We have been cooling off for a hundred years."* ✪ *The "Dr." was for King's Ph.D. in theology from Boston University.*

"Extremism in the Defense of Liberty Is No Vice."

Barry Goldwater, 1964

No presidential political campaign in the nation's history used fear more effectively than Lyndon Johnson's 1964 offensive against Senator Barry Goldwater. Democrat Johnson, who had been in the White House less than a year, was just putting together his social agenda, while simultaneously trying to figure out how to direct the fifteen thousand American forces over in Vietnam. A moderate Republican might easily have challenged his tenure, but reasonable discourse was not Goldwater's strong suit. At the GOP nominating convention, he set the tone for a campaign that would eventually do him in when he announced, "Moderation in the pursuit of justice is no virtue, and extremism in the defense of liberty is no vice." That speech gave the Democrats their biggest weapon—the "extremist" card—and they played it for all it was worth.

What Goldwater meant by extremism (or justice, or liberty) was never very clearly spelled out, because the Arizona senator betrayed a fatal propensity to shoot from the lip on a range of issues. He opposed virtually *all* social programs, from social security and the income tax to Johnson's promised "war on poverty"—which Goldwater called "as phony as a three-dollar bill." More generally, in time-honored conservative fashion, he was against Big Government but for Big Defense, and it was his potshots at the president's war policy that really destroyed his standing with middle-of-the-roaders. Branding Johnson's go-slow approach as a "no-win" policy, he hinted that, if elected, he would let field commanders use tactical nuclear weapons.

Having been handed this opening, the Democrats hardly needed to think. They quickly twisted the GOP's own slogan, "In your heart you know he's right," into two rewrites: "In your heart you know he's right—far right" and "In your guts you know he's nuts." They shrieked about the need for international restraint, even against Goldwater's nemesis, the "Communist conspiracy." They sold bumper stickers with the message "Help Barry Stamp Out Peace." And in a particularly effective pre-election TV ad, they showed a child playing merrily in a field of flowers—abruptly incinerated by a "Goldwater" nuclear explosion.

The fear of such warfare provided the Democratic slate with a massive winning margin. Goldwater took the Deep South and his own state. "Landslide Lyndon" took everything else, ending up with 61 percent of the popular vote and 486 out of 538 electoral votes. Goldwater went back to Arizona and was easily reelected to the Senate in 1968—by which time peace-loving Lyndon had sent half a million men to Vietnam.

TIDBITS: ✪ *The domestic villain in Goldwater's world view: the liberal press corps and liberal politicians, whom he ridiculed collectively as the "eastern establishment."* ✪ *Goldwater was nominated at the GOP convention by Richard Nixon.* ✪ *Best slogan mocking Barry's reactionism: "Goldwater in 1864."*

The Great Society
LBJ's domestic program, 1964–68

The modern American welfare state derives as much from Lyndon Johnson's five years in office as it does from his political mentor's New Deal. FDR provided mostly temporary solutions to the searing problems of the Great Depression; LBJ addressed systemic deficiencies, establishing a support structure for the chronically disadvantaged which he hoped would lead, in his sanguine terms, to a "Great Society."

LBJ took office on November 22, 1963, barely hours after the assassination of President Kennedy. He introduced the designation "Great Society" during the 1964 election campaign, but even before he defeated Barry Goldwater that November, he had begun the back-room lobbying at which he excelled to ensure the passage of his extraordinary social programs. Within a year after moving into the White House, he had succeeded where his elegant predecessor had failed, as Congress passed the broadest domestic program in thirty years.

Great Society legislation covered everything from conservation to education, from urban relief to housing support, but its major thrusts were at three related problems. The first was civil rights. Kennedy's sympathy with American blacks aside, JFK had not been able to marshal enough support in Congress to pass a sorely needed civil-rights act. The rough-hewn Johnson, a twenty-five-year veteran of congressional floor fights, cajoled and lectured his fellow southerners until they capitulated, and in 1964 he realized Kennedy's dream. Indeed, LBJ went it one better. Having outlawed discrimination in the Civil Rights Act, he secured the following year a Voting Rights Act, which attacked the technicalities that had kept blacks from the polls.

If racists blanched at this first facet of the Texan's plan, establishment medicine quaked at the second. The Medicare/Medicaid package, passed in 1965, provided health coverage for the elderly and the indigent, against the screechings of the American Medical Association and other lobbyists who warned that "socialized medicine" would soon be the order of the day. The entire superstructure of today's medical system—including, it must be admitted, its flagrant abuses—can be traced to LBJ's health initiatives.

The third, and most extensive, feature of the program was an attack on economic disadvantage, or—to put it positively—the promotion of broader opportunity. In his first State of the Union address, Johnson called for a nationwide "war on poverty." The Office of Economic Opportunity, founded in 1964, was to be staff headquarters for its campaigns. The OEO supervised, among other things, a young people's government-works program called the Job Corps, a domestic Peace Corps called Volunteers in Service to America (VISTA), the Head Start tutoring program for ghetto preschoolers, the college-prep Upward Bound program for their older siblings, sundry community-betterment projects, and job training. Congress earmarked just under a billion dollars for OEO's inaugural year and gradually was to up that amount at LBJ's urging.

The great campaign biographer Theodore White once guessed that "were there no outside world . . . Lyndon Johnson might conceivably have gone down as the greatest of twentieth-century presidents." LBJ's war on poverty alone justifies that assessment. But there *was* an outside world, filled with Vietnamese villages, napalm runs, and body bags. In the same year that his domestic programs got under way, the president also got the Gulf of Tonkin Resolution (see below). That resolution led to a deadly involvement that eventually forced LBJ's resignation as chief executive.

TIDBITS; ✪ *Before becoming Kennedy's vice-president, Johnson served twelve years in the House and another twelve in the Senate—the last six as majority leader.* ✪ *His wife, born Claudia Alta Taylor, called herself Lady Bird to please him. Their children were Luci Baines and Lynda Bird.* ✪ *Acid-rock queen Grace Slick of Jefferson Airplane first sang in a band called the Great Society.*

Gulf of Tonkin Resolution
August 10, 1964

Up until August 1964, U.S. involvement in Vietnam had been slight. After the French lost Indochina to the Communist Vietminh in 1954, the United States agreed to abide by peace accords that split the Vietnamese section of that country into a Communist North Vietnam and a non-Communist South Vietnam, controlled respectively by Ho Chi Minh and Ngo Dinh Diem. To support the Diem regime against Vietcong guerrillas, the Eisenhower administration sent a dribble of military advisers—less than seven hundred by the summer of 1960. JFK increased that commitment so dramatically—by the thousands—that *New York Times* correspondent James Reston was able to declare in February 1962 that the country had become involved in an "undeclared war." Still, the U.S. involvement was pretty small overall; by the time LBJ took office in November 1963, only sixteen thousand American personnel had been committed.

What cranked this investment up a quantum leap—and sucked the nation into what many called "the quagmire"—was alleged North Vietnamese attacks on U.S. destroyers in the embattled country's Gulf of Tonkin. I say "alleged" because a Senate investigation mounted later found that the incidents' gravity may have been blown out of proportion, and that one of them may not even have happened at all. Nobody, however, suspected the credibility of the account when LBJ spoke to the nation on August 5, announcing retaliatory bombings against North Vietnam and asking Congress, after the fact, to approve his action.

The resulting Gulf of Tonkin Resolution—passed with only two dissenting votes in the Senate, none in the House—gave the president carte blanche to do whatever he deemed necessary to protect American lives *and* (in a portentous rider) to take "all necessary steps, including the use of armed force," to protect Southeast Asia Treaty Organization (SEATO) pact countries from external aggression. Even though South Vietnam at the time wasn't a member of that pact, and even though its government had not requested further U.S. aid, Johnson read the resolution as an imprimatur for wider war and started an immediate beefing-up of American involvement. Within six months U.S. troop numbers there had tripled, and within a year they had passed 150,000.

The Senate investigation that cast doubt on LBJ's picture of the Tonkin attacks came in 1968. By that time the North Vietnamese capital, Hanoi, was being bombed almost daily, nearly half a million U.S. men and women had been sent to Vietnam, and the American public had become gruesomely accustomed to seeing flag-draped coffins and body counts on the evening news. The North Vietnamese "Tet offensive" of that year, which visited heavy losses on the American-backed South, led to a bombing halt, preliminary peace feelers, and Johnson's decision, announced on March 31, not to seek another term in office. But it would be another year, and under another president, before troop pullouts began in earnest. By the time Saigon, the capital of South Vietnam, finally fell to the Vietcong in 1975, effectively ending the war, the quagmire had taken over fifty-eight thousand American lives, and an untold number of Vietnamese.

TIDBITS: ✪ *The U.S. destroyers supposedly attacked in August of 1964:* Maddox *and* Turner Joy. ✪ *The two dissenting votes: Oregon's Wayne Morse, Alaska's Ernest Gruening.* ✪ *Head of the 1965 committee that investigated the Tonkin incident: Arkansas senator William Fulbright, initiator of the student- and teacher-exchange Fulbright Scholarships.*

"Don't Trust Anyone Over Thirty."

"Counterculture" slogan, 1960s

The youth culture of the 1960s was nothing if not loquacious. More memorable slogans came out of that decade's "counterculture movement" than out of any other American decade since the Civil War. The theme that tied them all together was youthful rebellion, as expressed memorably in the decade's most egregiously adolescent announcement, "Don't trust anyone over thirty." But within that theme there were two major subtexts, reflecting a frequently observed division between "politicos" and "druggies."

The focus of the political sloganeering was the Vietnam War, and more broadly the allegedly imperialist Establishment that was prosecuting it. The United States has never been engaged in a less popular war than the Vietnam incursion, and the antiwar slogans of the era reflected the broad base of the opposition.

Idealogues spoke of smashing fascist "Amerika" and replacing it with socialist people's republics. Other leftists, such as the members of Students for a Democratic Society, took over university buildings, burned draft cards, and issued proclamations, such as SDS's own Port Huron Statement, calling for the implementation of "participatory democracy." Radical blacks, aware that their brothers were doing most of the grunt work in Vietnam, said, "No Vietnamese ever called me nigger," and denounced a war where "black men kill yellow men to protect land that white men stole from red men." And war resisters of various persuasions united behind the chants "Hell no, we won't go!" and the taunting "Hey, hey, LBJ, how many kids did you kill today?"

The results of this activism were significant. On college campuses and in city squares, opposition to the war escalated along with the bombing of North Vietnam, while in such demonstrations as the 1967 peace march on the Pentagon and 1969's nationwide Vietnam Moratorium, it became evident that public support for administration policies was growing thin. Sixties activism, as much as the "unwinnability" of the war itself, led to President Johnson's 1968 decision not to seek a second term, and to the ultimate withdrawal of U.S. forces from Southeast Asia.

The results of the less political, more drug-oriented sloganeering were not as clear. The "acid freaks" and "potheads" of the sixties shared the political activists' antipathy to the Establishment, but their response to "systemic repression" was generally more private, and certainly more hedonistic and self-indulgent. Following Harvard-professor-turned-LSD-guru Timothy Leary, they sought release from a materialist culture in "hippie" clothing, in generally ill-fated attempts at going "back to the land," in a public flouting of their "uptight" parents' mores, and in unique combinations of Eastern religions and Western sensuality.

The general lassitude of the counterculture's chemical contingent was reflected in the blissful openness of its recommendations. These included relatively specific endorsements of the pleasure principle—"Sex, drugs, and rock 'n' roll," "Make love, not war," and "If it moves, fondle it"—as well as Leary's famous call to lysergic-acid paradise, "Tune in, turn on, drop out." But other recommendations were boldly empty of data: In the blissed-out looseness of the time, perhaps the most typical non-political admonition was the deliciously bland "Do your own thing."

Since so many young people's "own thing" involved the ingestion of mind-altering chemicals, it's hardly surprising that the counterculture's drug wing produced less obvious results than the radical leftists. San Francisco, birthplace of the hippie phenomenon, generated various "love-ins" and a "Summer of Love," while on a New York state farm in August 1969, the Woodstock Festival drew half a million young people to celebrate "three days of peace and music." Although the lasting effects of the era's psychedelic consciousness are hard to measure, for both druggies and politicos "Woodstock Nation" remains a vivid symbol of a generation's dreams.

TIDBITS: ✪ *Prefeminist antiwar slogan: "Girls say yes to boys who say no."* ✪ *Conservative response to war protesters:*

"America, love it or leave it" and *"If your heart isn't in America, get your ass out."* ✪ *Author of the "over thirty" line: Jack Weinberg, of Berkeley's Free Speech movement.*

"Black Power"

Militant activist slogan, 1960s

Even before Martin Luther King, Jr., was assassinated at a Memphis motel in 1968, fissures had begun to develop in the nonviolent civil-rights movement he started. In 1964, King's people had worked closely with members of the Student Nonviolent Coordinating Committee ("Snick") to register black voters in rural Mississippi, but shortly thereafter SNCC chairman Stokely Carmichael led his followers on an increasingly separatist course, rejecting integration and nonviolence as counterproductive. About the same time, a fiery orator named Malcolm Little joined the Black Muslims, changed his name to Malcolm X, and began espousing the group's doctrine of self-sufficiency. In Oakland, California, Bobby Seale and Huey Newton formed the militant separatist group the Black Panthers; sporting rifles on their hips and "Afro" haircuts, the Panthers spawned similar groups around the country dedicated to self-rule, or "Black Power," for ghetto communities.

By 1968, such nonaccommodationist, visibly angry young blacks were already public threats to King's goals. When King fell to a sniper's bullet that April, their radical solutions suddenly seemed reasonable by default. Thousands of young blacks, mostly in the northern inner cities, vented their frustrations in a wave of grief-filled violence. While acid-happy hippies were enjoying a Summer of Love in San Francisco, young blacks in Newark, New Jersey, and Los Angeles were torching their own neighborhoods and looting white stores. Charges of police brutality were raised daily. Marxist theoretician Angela Davis spoke out in defense of a violent overthrow of an unsalvageable system. In the presidential election of that year, the Panthers—in concert with the white Peace and Freedom Party—ran Eldridge Cleaver on a "revolution now" platform. At Cornell University in 1969, black students armed themselves against "white intimidation" and for two days occupied the student union.

These new, more confrontational activists addressed the cultural as well as the economic aspects of racism. Rejecting their elders' attempts to fit into white society, they donned dashikis and other expressions of their African heritage, taught the ideal of "black pride" to children in community schools, fought for black-studies programs on college campuses, and—echoing a phrase that had first been used by black nationalist Marcus Garvey in the 1920s—declared that "black is beautiful." To build up a strong economic base in their own communities, the Black Panthers ran free clinics and meal programs, while fighting broadly for black ownership of ghetto businesses.

Little of this positive work was visible to mainstream America, since the press preferred to concentrate on getting young blacks bearing arms. And those radical leaders themselves did little to dispel the fear their image created. The Panthers posed theatrically in black leather jackets and military-style berets, and Carmichael's successor as SNCC chairman, H. Rap Brown, was to quip, "Violence is as American as apple pie." True enough, but not an attitude exactly designed to win you allies.

By the beginning of the 1970s, Black Power, like most other radical alternatives to the supposedly moribund "system," had become worn out, or—in some cases—shot out. Malcolm X, after a split with Muslim leader Elijah Muhammad, was killed (evidently by rival Muslims) at a Harlem rally in 1965. After several well-publicized gun battles with police, most Panther leaders were either arrested, legally murdered, or forced into exile. Chicago police killed two of that city's Panther leaders in their sleep; Bobby Seale went on trial with the Chicago Eight (see below), and Eldridge Cleaver, whose book *Soul on Ice* was a literary bible for the movement, fled the country to seek a haven in socialist Algeria. At the same time, with the election of several black mayors, the focus of power seemed to be returning to the moderate center.

TIDBITS: ✪ *Where-Are-They-Now-Department: Bobby Seale works with a youth-employment project in Philadelphia. Angela Davis teaches black studies and women's studies in California. Eldridge Cleaver is a born-again Christian.* ✪ *The country's first black mayor: Carl Stokes, Cleveland, 1967.*

The Chicago Eight

Chicago conspiracy trial, 1969–70

In August 1968, the Democratic Party descended on the city of Chicago to nominate a successor to Lyndon B. Johnson, who had shocked the nation six months earlier by announcing he would not seek a second term. Since the Democrats were still waging the Vietnam War, which had in effect forced Johnson out of office, various dissidents decided to convene on the convention in a massive no-confidence vote. Resulting street clashes between demonstrators and the Chicago police led to the arrest of eight "leaders" for inciting a riot. Put on trial between September 1969 and February 1970, they became known as the Chicago Eight. In the order of the grand jury indictment, they were:

✪ David Dellinger, a longtime pacifist and an organizer of the 1967 March on the Pentagon;

✪ Rennie Davis, an SDS community organizer (see page 198) and member of the National Mobilization Committee against the war;

✪ Tom Hayden, Davis's fellow SDSer and the principal author of the group's manifesto, the Port Huron Statement;

✪ Abbie Hoffman, a "cultural revolutionary" who had helped found the playfully anarchistic Youth International Party (the Yippies) and had recently mocked the U.S. economic system by throwing money away at the New York Stock Exchange;

✪ Jerry Rubin, Hoffman's fellow Yippie, who had worked in Berkeley's Free Speech movement and with Dellinger on the Pentagon march;

✪ John Froines, another SDSer, who had worked in black community organizing and in 1968 was teaching chemistry at the University of Oregon;

✪ Lee Weiner, another teacher, then working on a sociology doctorate at Northwestern; and

✪ Bobby Seale, cofounder and chairman of the Oakland-based Black Panther party.

All eight were tried under the so-called Rap Brown law, an antiriot provision in the 1968 Civil Rights Act named for the SNCC leader who, conservatives believed, had incited riots the year before. The first six were also charged with speaking to various "assemblages of persons" with an eye to "inciting, organizing, promoting, and encouraging a riot," while Froines and Weiner were said to have taught their students how to use "incendiary devices."

The trial of the Eight, in writer Samuel Krislov's felicitous phrasing, "encapsulated the dialectics of an era." The defendants, convinced they were political prisoners, took ample opportunity to use the journalist-thick courtroom as a soapbox, condemning not only the war, but also the moral limitations of "fascist," "racist," or simply "pig" America. The judge, stiff-necked and blatantly biased Julius Hoffman, was just as determined that his fief should remain "in order," and the inevitable conflict was by turns sobering and hilarious. Among the highlights of the circuslike proceedings were the defendants' draping of Vietcong and American flags over the defense table, the shackling and gagging of defendant Seale after repeated outbursts, and a bewildering number of contempt rulings and cries of "Pig!"

Given the political climate of Chicago, and the suspicion that Judge Hoffman had permitted a biased jury, the Eight's convictions were perhaps inevitable. Even so, the jurors were aware that the government's case for conspiracy was shaky— "We couldn't agree on lunch," laughed Abbie Hoffman—and that a federal commission, in its Walker Report, had said the "riot" in question was actually caused by the police. In the end, the conspiracy charge didn't stick. But Dellinger, Davis, Hayden, Hoffman, and Rubin each got five years for their inflammatory speeches. Froines and Weiner were found not guilty, and Seale got off on a mistrial.

But Judge Hoffman also imposed lavish contempt sentences on the defendants—*and* on their "disorderly" counsel. Chief defender William Kunstler alone racked up more than 140 citations. To radical observers, the contempt citations proved that the government was merely using the Rap Brown law to prosecute the expression of dissent. An appeals court agreed, reversing Judge Hoffman's judgment on all but three defendants.

In a parting shot, Jerry Rubin inscribed a copy of his book *Do It!* to the judge. "Dear Julius," it read, "the demonstrations in Chicago in 1968 were the first steps in the revolution. What happened in the courtroom is the second step. Julius, you radicalized more young people than we ever could. You're the country's top Yippie." Maybe. But what really "radicalized" more youth as the seventies started were the U.S. invasion of

Vietcong enemy "sanctuaries" in Vietnam's neighbor Cambodia; the killing of six college students during demonstrations at Ohio's Kent State and Florida's Jackson State; the court-martial of army lieutenant William Calley for the murder of Vietnamese civilians; and publication of the so-called Pentagon Papers, which detailed official deception regarding the running of the war.

TIDBITS: ✪ *Immediate outcome of the Chicago demonstrations: the election defeat of the tainted Democratic party and its candidate, Minnesota's Hubert Humphrey.* ✪ *Yippie candidate for president, 1968: Pigasus, a four-hundred-pound pig.* ✪ *Other news, 1969: Neil Armstrong walks on the moon.*

"An Effete Corps of Impudent Snobs"

Spiro T. Agnew, 1969

When the Watergate scandal (see page 209) brought the Nixon administration to its knees, many Republicans blamed a "hounding" press for blowing the "third-rate burglary" out of proportion. For more than a decade, Nixon had enjoyed no better than an adversary relationship with journalists, and his supporters saw the *Washington Post*'s revelations as just the last in a string of liberal attacks. So poor was the president's rapport with the media, in fact, that press conferences during his term were rare as eclipses, and Nixon himself was seldom seen in a public forum that was not protectively packed with supporters of his Vietnam War aims. Since somebody had to talk to the cameras, Nixon delegated the unpleasant task to his vice-president—which made the Greek moniker Spiro Agnew a household name.

As Maryland's law-and-order governor in the 1960s, Agnew had managed to escape the national limelight—so much so that, when Nixon chose him as running mate, even Republicans scratched their heads, asking "Spiro who?" But soon after taking office as vice-president, and until his resignation four years later, Agnew spoke to scores of civic, trade, and political groups, gaining a quick—and increasingly controversial—reputation as the scourge of liberal thinking in all its guises. With steadfast loyalty to Nixon's conservative policies and a flair for alliteration, Agnew attacked with equal venom student protesters, antiwar congressmen, and the press "Establishment" which, in his view, consistently distorted both the president's policy and public opinion.

To Agnew, student protesters were worse than misguided. With their intolerance for opposing views, they threatened democracy itself; the "persistent street struggles" of the 1960s were a sign of "degeneracy," of a drift toward a system in which the "voice of the mob" dictated public policy. Liberal "elitists" were no better. Their "permissive prattle" about free speech disguised the reality that "obscenity-chanting young dissidents" were destroying the country. Worst of all was the eastern "fraternity" that had monopolized communication; in the vice-president's view, the TV networks, the *Washington Post*, and the *New York Times* were depriving the public by presenting their "radical-liberal" picture of current events as "objective" reality.

Agnew's war with the press began in earnest after a Des Moines speech in November 1969, in which he denounced the small clique of TV producers and commentators whose editorial choices determined "what forty to fifty million Americans will learn of the day's events." For the next four years, as Nixon played cat-and-mouse with the North Vietnamese, Agnew kept up a bantering exchange with these unelected tastemakers, calling them, among other things, "nattering nabobs of negativism" and "an effete corps of impudent snobs." They responded by charging the Nixon administration with indirect censorship. Agnew retaliated by calling them the censors.

So it went, with Middle America enjoying the vice-president's intemperance as much as the liberal opposition hated it, until the summer of 1973, when Agnew made the startling disclosure that he was being investigated on suspicion of bribery and tax evasion. In October, the one Nixon high official who had somehow managed to escape the Watergate brush pled "no contest" to the latter charge and abruptly resigned the vice-presidency. The media breathed a collective sigh of relief, although the issues that Agnew raised regarding its liberal bias have resurfaced under subsequent Republican tenures.

TIDBITS: ✪ *The "nattering nabobs" called him Spiro, but to his friends he went by his middle name, Ted.* ✪ *In Communist Peking, Agnew was known as "the God of Plague."* ✪ *Many memorable "Agnewisms" were penned by Republican speechwriter (and later* New York Times *columnist) William Safire.* ✪ *The only other vice-presidential resignee: John C. Calhoun, who left Andrew Jackson's administration (see page 63) in 1832.*

"I Am Not a Crook."
Richard M. Nixon, 1974

Throughout most of his career "Tricky Dick" Nixon was the favorite whipping boy of American liberals, not only because of his blatant Left-baiting, but because his conservatism seemed opportunistic. He initially established a reputation as a "sneak" in 1946, when he won a California congressional seat by depicting his opponent, laborite Jerry Voorhis, as controlled by the state's "Commie" labor unions. Two years later he gained a national anti-Red reputation by grilling suspected spy Alger Hiss in televised House Un-American Activities Committee hearings. In 1950, he made it to the Senate, using the same tactics against opponent Helen Gahagan Douglas that had given him his victory over Voorhis.

As Dwight Eisenhower's running mate in 1952, Nixon fended off a corruption charge by explaining that a secret slush fund wealthy backers had set up for him was actually designed to save taxpayers money. As if that tortuous logic weren't enough, he added to the impression of disingenuousness by claiming that his wife wore "a good Republican cloth coat" and that—no matter how loud the Democrats yelled—he was not going to return the little dog, Checkers, that a political supporter had given his children as a present. Nixon rode Ike's coattails into the vice-presidency, but the "Checkers speech" gave comedians material for the next eight years.

Nixon went for the presidency in 1960 and lost narrowly to JFK. Two years later, when he lost the California governor's race to Pat Brown, he told a generally pleased press corps, "You won't have Nixon to kick around anymore." He kept that promise for six years, working tirelessly for Republican candidates while hiring media consultants to help him polish his image. In 1968 a "new Nixon"—ostensibly more amiable and straightforward—emerged, and in November he took the presidential election from Hubert Humphrey.

As president, of course, he inherited the Vietnam War that had forced his predecessor, Lyndon Johnson, out of office. Those who felt Nixon was inherently two-faced felt vindicated when the Republican "peace" candidate ordered the invasion of Cambodia in April 1970 and the notorious Christmas bombing of North Vietnam in 1972. Nixon did, however, gradually pull out the troops, reaching agreements on paper with the Hanoi regime in 1973. On the wider front, he also surprised people when he began arms talks with the hated Russkies and visited the Communist citadels of Moscow and Peking.

But then came Watergate. In the summer of 1972, as Nixon was mounting a reelection campaign against Democratic challenger George McGovern, five men were arrested after breaking into Democratic committee headquarters in Washington's Watergate building. It seemed they had been sent there by Nixon's private campaign consultancy, the Committee to Reelect the President (affectionately known as CREEP). Nixon denied any connection between the White House and the "third-rate burglary," but the press—especially the *Washington Post*'s Bob Woodward and Carl Bernstein—wouldn't let it go, and shortly after Nixon was reelected in November, a web of deceit began to unravel. Not only had CREEP sent the creeps, but also (a) the White House had a secret "plumbers" group designed to plug leaks and investigate "subversives"; (b) at least one of the burglars, E. Howard Hunt, Jr., had been sent hush money by somebody in the White House; (c) the brain behind the break-in was Nixon's attorney general, John Mitchell.

There was, distressingly, a lot more of the same. To extinguish rumors that the White House was involved in this mess, Nixon appointed a special prosecutor, Archibald Cox, to investigate the case. But when Cox asked Nixon himself to surrender tapes of conversations he had recorded in the White House, the president demurred, citing "executive privilege," and replaced him with a new prosecutor, Leon Jaworski. The tapes quickly became the center of the controversy, with Nixon's critics convinced they were a "smoking gun" that would place the president in charge of a cover-up. In good old Tricky Dick style, Nixon first released edited transcripts of the tapes, then tapes containing supposedly accidental erasures. "What did Nixon know?" became the newspapers' favorite headline of 1974, with presidential activity totally hamstrung by the Watergate fiasco.

By that summer, impeachment hearings were under way, and it seemed certain that Nixon would be removed from office for obstruction of justice. He sidestepped the inevitable by re-signing. He never did spell out what he knew, or when he knew it, although before he left he did give the public the blanket assurance, "I am not a crook." His family—and three or four others—seemed to believe him. His vice-president, Gerald Ford, may or may not have believed him, but in any event, one month after succeeding to the presidency, he granted his former boss a "full, free, and absolute pardon" for anything he "may have" done between 1969 and 1974.

T I D B I T S : ✪ *Best study of the media-manufactured "new Nixon": Joe McGinniss's* The Selling of the President. ✪ *Nixon was first implicated in the Watergate cover-up by his own presidential counsel, John Dean III.* ✪ *Nixon secretary responsible for "accidentally" erasing eighteen minutes of poten-tially incriminating conversation: Rosemary Woods.* ✪ *Federal judge in charge of the case: John J. Sirica.*

"Tie a Yellow Ribbon Round the Old Oak Tree."

Iranian hostage crisis, 1979–81

No question about what did Jimmy Carter in. During his administration, on the home front, the Baptist boy from Plains, Georgia, had not only restored a sense of integrity to the Oval Office after the Watergate debacle, but he had spoken forcefully to the nation's ongoing dilemmas: in his tenure both energy and education were taken seriously enough to be addressed by newly created cabinet departments. Abroad, in spite of his inexperience, Georgia's former governor had racked up an impressive record of wins, including a treaty for the peaceful transferral of the Panama Canal Zone back to its original owners, arms-limitation talks with the Soviets, and—most memorably—the steady cajoling of Israel's and Egypt's leaders into a peace accord; this was signed at the presidential retreat, Camp David, in 1979. But one nut—the Iranian revolution—he could not crack, and it was that failure that lost him his office.

The trouble started decades before Carter's time, in previous administrations' strategic chumminess with Iran's Shah. Although the Shah's regime had an appalling human-rights record, a stable Iran was considered geographically critical to American interests in the oil-rich Middle East, so when Islamic revolutionaries forced the Shah out in 1979, human-rights champion Carter ironically followed the lead of his predecessors and refused to repudiate the nation's longtime friend. Indeed, so uncomfortably cozy did Carter remain that the ailing Shah chose the United States for asylum—as much for its medical facilities as for its friendship. The decision to admit him that October led to mob attacks on the U.S. embassy in Teheran, the capture of more than fifty hostages by the revolutionaries, Carter's freezing of Iranian assets in retaliation, and a subsequent war of nerves that lasted 444 days.

During that period, as Carter's people negotiated behind the scenes, the American landscape began to resemble a macabre parade route, as thousands of citizens, following the lead of one hostage's wife, draped yellow ribbons around trees and fence posts as a sign of solidarity with the pawns overseas. In the waning years of the Vietnam War, the popular song "Tie a Yellow Ribbon Round the Old Oak Tree" had celebrated a wife's faithfulness to her imprisoned lover, so this symbol was poignantly appropriate to the hostage crisis. (The symbol reappeared with a vengeance during the 1991 Gulf War, when it stood for solidarity with U.S. troops.)

In April 1980, with negotiations stalled, Carter tried a military option to rescue the hostages. The resulting Delta Force fiasco, in which mechanical failures and poor judgment led to the loss of eight rescuers' lives, was the low point of Carter's perceived effectiveness and a trump card in the Republicans' attack on his leadership. They also cited his go-slow, talk-it-out policy as proof of his incompetence.

In the end the hostages did come home—shattered by the experience but none permanently damaged, at least physically. They were released, by no mere coincidence, on Ronald Reagan's inauguration day, January 20, 1981. Explanations for the timing of the release vary. Was Iranian leader Ayatollah Khomeini so angered by the botched rescue attempt that he sought to add insult to injury, giving Reagan the kudos Carter had really earned? Was he afraid of the tough-talking Californian—fearful that, if he hesitated any longer, Reagan's bite might prove as bad as his bark? Or was there a deal cut? Are Reagan's critics right in suggesting that his people arranged for the detention of the hostages to secure the election, in exchange for arms sales to the hostage-takers? As of 1992, this final theory is still being debated.

What's clear is that Carter lost the election and went down in history, at least temporarily, as a loser. It's an ill-fitting mantle for the author of the Camp David accords, and one that will surely be reassessed as time goes on. A more generous appraisal comes from James Berber, a political scientist at Duke University. "When a president leaves office with the Constitution more or less intact, and without a lot of dead American boys scattered around the planet," Berber says, "we ought to give him a medal."

T I D B I T S : ✪ *Carter's other international headache was the U.S.S.R.'s 1979 invasion of Afghanistan. Responses included the so-called Carter Doctrine, which warned the Soviets away from control of the Persian Gulf; and the U.S. boycott of the 1980 Moscow Olympics.* ✪ *Other news, 1979: Nuclear power-plant explosion at Pennsylvania's Three Mile Island.* ✪ *Other news, 1980: Eruption of Mount St. Helens volcano.*

"I Think it Was a Neat Idea."

Oliver North, 1987

For most of Ronald Reagan's time on Pennsylvania Avenue, the former actor enjoyed a honeymoon with the press and public that engendered the phrase "Teflon presidency." When the president dozed or daydreamed through meetings, it was put down as a charming quirk. When he visited a Nazi burial plot in Germany, most writers forgot about it within weeks. When he tested a microphone at a press conference by joking, "We begin bombing [the Soviet Union] in ten minutes," he was seen as a card, not a clod. When hundreds of U.S. Marines died in a bomb attack in Beirut, Reagan's ultimate responsibility as commander in chief was barely mentioned. Hence "Teflon"; criticism simply didn't stick to him—until his eleventh-hour implication in "Iran/Contra."

The basic facts of the bizarre episode were as follows: Around the summer of 1986, under the direction of a charismatic Marine colonel named Oliver North, America sold certain missiles and other arms to Iran to help in its war with Iraq. Since Iran was on this country's official non-grata list—we thought of it, with good reason, as a haven for terrorists—the deal was made in secret, and with a twist. In addition to the Iranians making a cash payment, they would also use their leverage in the Middle East to secure the release of American hostages held in Lebanon by terrorist groups sympathetic to their Islamic revolution. Naturally, this "arms for hostages" deal had to be concealed from the American public.

But there was more. While Americans were being held hostage in Lebanon, a threat to freedom was also perceived in our own hemisphere. Recognizing that fact, the president in 1983 had ordered the invasion of the tiny Caribbean island of Grenada, to cleanse it of a government friendly to Fidel Castro. But there was still Nicaragua, which, since 1979, had been under the rule of the Communist Sandinistas. In turn, they had been under attack by counterrevolutionaries known as the Contras. Wouldn't it be great, somebody suggested to Colonel North, if we could use some of the money coming from Iran to support these "freedom fighters" in our own backyard? Absolutely, he responded—a terrific plan. Or, as he later put it to a Senate investigation, he thought it was "a neat idea."

One problem: it was illegal. Since the Contras had been implicated in activities ranging from drug smuggling to rape and murder, popular support for them in this country was eroding, and in 1982 the Boland Amendment, introduced by Massachusetts congressman Edward Boland, flatly prohibited federal support for the Contra cause. It was widely known that Reagan wanted them supported, but presidential desire is not the same thing as law.

Unless your name is Oliver North. Knowing what his chief wanted him to do—even if the old man couldn't legally come out and say it—North engineered a covert operation to divert arms-sale funds to Nicaragua in spite of Boland. The discovery of this operation—which included an international network of arms dealers and go-betweens—led in the summer of 1987 to the most enthralling Senate hearings since Joe McCarthy's day. They included appearances by not only the ramrod colonel, but also by his immediate superior, national security chief John Poindexter; by his secretary, Fawn Hall, who admitted shredding incriminating documents at North's suggestion; and by a host of bit players in the international deception, ranging from straightforward mercenaries to zealots like North himself, who believed that it was the president, and not the Congress, who made foreign policy.

At issue here were two critical questions. One was the Constitutional question of executive versus legislative power, which the Congress interpreted quite differently from Colonel North, feeling (oddly) that even the president was not above the law. The second question was one of fact: how much did Reagan know? If he flat-out authorized Poindexter and North to ignore the Boland Amendment, then he had obstructed justice and was as ripe for impeachment as Richard Nixon had been. On the other hand, if he didn't know about the diversion of funds, he was guilty at the very least of poor management.

To find out what the president knew, Congress invited him to testify, but the most they could get out of him was a string of "don't recalls" and "wasn't awares." Ollie and John *thought* he knew, but they couldn't prove it. Unlike Watergate, the Contra caper had no smoking gun. So North and Poindexter got a year each; the sentences were suspended and later overturned on appeal—and Reagan, still the consummate actor, escaped the last and most grievous threat to his Teflon armor. The worst that anyone could say with certainty about his role in the funds diversion was that he was not sufficiently in control of the situation. Liberals had been saying that for seven years.

TIDBITS: ✪ *For his part in the obstruction of justice, Colonel North became a folk hero; those who admired his fervent anti-Communism even proposed him as a presidential possibility.* ✪ *If*

North had never received an okay from the president himself, then the next highest-up approval could have come from CIA director William Casey, who died halfway through the hearings. ✪ *Common nicknames for the episode: Iranscam, Iranamuck, Contragate.*

"A Kinder and Gentler Nation"

George Bush, 1988

The 1988 presidential election campaign was not one of the more salubrious on record. Ostensibly a contest between the big-defense/small-domestic-budget policy of the Republicans and the trim-defense/welfare-state stance of the Democrats, it quickly degenerated, with both incumbent vice-president George Bush and Massachusetts governor Michael Dukakis concentrating on attacking the character of the other. Voters were not amused. A popular bumper sticker suggested "Nobody for President."

As the candidate with a national record to defend—and perhaps more to be defensive about—Bush went on the attack early, calling the obvious breaking-down of the Soviet system a Republican accomplishment and ingeniously blaming Mr. Reagan's trillion-dollar budget on the forty years of Democratic New Dealism (see page 161) that had preceded it. Then, alert to charges that Reagan's gutting of social programs had hurt the poor, he promised that his election would bring a "kinder and gentler nation," not through tax-supported government spending (the Democrats' failed solution) but through greater volunteerism in the private sector—the people-helping-each-other approach that he characterized as "a thousand points of light."

Dukakis, as severe as Bush was chipper, claimed credit for the high-employment "Massachusetts Miracle," promised a "sound" rather than a huge defense network, and admitted—with an honesty that probably killed him—that he couldn't second Bush's pledge of "no new taxes." As for the thousand points of light, he admitted sardonically, "I don't know what that means."

Then the sniping really started. Using a time-tested law-and-order tactic, Bush accused the Massachusetts governor of being soft on criminals, using as evidence the notorious case of Willie Horton, a Bay State murderer who had won early release from prison on a Dukakis furlough program—and used his freedom to commit a rape. In television ads, the Bush campaign hinted that a Dukakis White House would flood our streets with roving maniacs. On top of that, Bush declared that the "Duke" knew nothing of foreign policy; that his "miracle" was a coattail effect of the Reagan boom; and—worst of all—that he, like so many liberals, was a "card-carrying member of the ACLU," implying that the defense of civil liberties meant the coddling of a criminal element.

Astonishingly, Dukakis took this lying down until it was too late in the campaign to undo it. Rather than proclaiming "Yes, I'm a liberal, and proud of it," he let the Bush offensive set the agenda to such an extent that "the L word" actually became a campaign issue. When he did come back, it was not to analyze Reagan's domestic failures, but to trade character assassination with character assassination. Putting economics aside, Dukakis hammered at the vice-president's involvement in the supposed "arms for hostages" deal of two years before. Bush's disingenuous statement that he was not privy to any such negotiations ("out of the loop" was how he put it) was, evidently, bought by the public.

Bush won, of course, and gave us the "kinder and gentler" America we enjoy today. Dukakis, who had campaigned for the Oval Office while still governor, finished out his term and then retired from Bay State politics in 1990—just as his "miracle" began to crumble around everyone's ears. In 1991 "Taxachusetts" ranked dead last among the fifty states in per-capita income, and her former governor became only slightly more popular than Saddam Hussein.

TIDBITS: ✪ *Proof that the "one heartbeat away from the presidency" argument doesn't guarantee anything: Bush's running mate, the jejune Hoosier J. Danforth Quayle.* ✪ *Best conservative nickname for the government-heavy Bay State: the People's Republic of Massachusetts.*

"The Liberation of Kuwait Has Begun."

George Bush, January 17, 1991

The roots of the brief war known as Desert Storm lay in the troubled soil of the Iranian revolution. When Islamic fundamentalists forced the Shah from his throne in 1979, President Carter, who had done so well at Camp David (see page 211), faltered badly, embracing the Shah and thus alienating the new rulers. They were so alienated, in fact, that they took more than fifty U.S. hostages, whom they kept in painful isolation for a year and a half. When neighboring Iraq then invaded Iran in 1984, the Reagan regime practiced post-facto revenge, standing by while U.S. allies armed the Iraqis in the hope of a reduced Iran or a power standoff. For forty years American policy in the Mideast had hung on maintaining a balance of power among competing neighbors; backing the perceived underdog in the Iran-Iraq war was in line with this view.

But Iraq soon became the overdog—so much so that by the end of Reagan's term the country's ruler, Saddam Hussein, had created the fourth largest army in the world. By the end of the 1980s, the balance of terror had shifted, and the United States was left in the unenviable position of having to halt a threat to which its own policies had contributed. The situation was complicated, moreover, by the fact that Saddam Hussein controlled major oil supplies—and was eyeing those of his neighbor, wealthy Kuwait.

When Iraq invaded Kuwait in August 1990, President Bush's initial response was straightforward and pragmatic. We were against aggression, he told the public, for two reasons: because it was aggression and because it threatened "our way of life"—meaning that with Saddam Hussein in charge of Kuwaiti oil, we'd be even harder-pressed than during past oil crises to keep our outboard motors and air-conditioners humming. But as 1990 turned into 1991, with reports of Iraqi atrocities in Kuwait making front-page news, the humanitarian rationale soon outpaced economic concerns, and the idea of American intervention to liberate the occupied kingdom was presented, more and more, as "the right thing to do."

Since the rest of the industrialized world also needed oil, and since few people had good words for Saddam Hussein, Bush was able, between August and January, to pull together a remarkable United Nations coalition—twenty-nine nations in all—dedicated to the liberation of tiny Kuwait. Amazingly, after the coalition's offensive against Saddam began on January 16, the Arab members of this group stuck to it even though Saddam made desperate attempts to fracture the bond by involving the Arabs' traditional enemy, Israel, in the conflagration.

In the United States, Desert Storm was preceded by the

most intense and eloquent congressional debate since the Compromise of 1850. It ended on January 13 with Congress granting the president, by a slim margin, a mandate for force. Three days later the first bombers hit Baghdad, and the next morning Bush announced the "liberation." From there on the coalition dominated, enjoying a month of air superiority, another few days of lightning ground battles, the chasing of Iraqi forces back into their own country, and a cease-fire by early March. The coalition's limited war aim—removing Saddam Hussein from Kuwait—was accomplished with minimal allied losses, and Mr. Bush's popularity rating went up to 83 percent—the highest rating ever attained by a U.S. executive.

The popularity of the war aside, the Gulf region suffered major casualties. Even the surgically precise bombing of which American technocrats were so proud left countless Iraqis, military and civilian, maimed or dead. Several months after the U.N. victory, hundreds of oil fields that the Iraqi army had set afire were still burning. Kurds in northern Iraq, encouraged to rebel by the U.S. president, were brutally repressed by Saddam's soldiers when they did so. Not least of all, a restive Iran enjoyed the fruits of a shifted power balance it had gotten for free. In the midst of the postwar euphoria that swept Bush's America, only the cynical seemed to notice that the aims we had fought for—self-determination and cheap oil—were no more secure than they had ever been.

TIDBITS: ✪ *The January 13 Senate proposal authorizing the immediate use of force passed by a vote of 52 to 47.* ✪ *Most visible war hero, and touted candidate for Bush's successor: the operation's overall commander, "Stormin' " Norman Schwarzkopf.* ✪ *Most visible domestic expression of troop support: yellow ribbons around a million trees.*

Appendix I

Words We Voted By

Presidents don't get to the White House on the basis of one-liners alone, but a good one never kept anybody out. Since 1840, when songs and slogans first helped to determine a national election, phrasemakers have been as crucial as policy-makers—sometimes more so—in defining the contending parties' appeal. A few of their campaign zingers have even outlived the issues that generated them, to become part of the nation's political folklore. Here are twelve of the best.

"Tippecanoe and Tyler Too"

Whig slogan, 1840

In the nation's first "singing campaign," the Whig nominee was Indiana's William Henry Harrison, who had narrowly beaten Tecumseh's Creek warriors at the Battle of Tippecanoe in 1811; his running mate was Virginian John Tyler. After being depicted by the incumbent Democrats as a cider-swilling rustic, Harrison allowed his handlers to manipulate the image to his advantage; they set up log-cabin campaign posts throughout the country, complete with free cider for voters. Among the many down-home ditties that painted the wealthy Harrison as a man of the people, Alexander Ross's "Tip and Ty" was among the most popular. Its chorus, "Tippecanoe and Tyler too," became the Whigs' most effective campaign slogan, moving the sixty-eight-year-old war hero into the White House—where he stayed for one month before succumbing to pneumonia.

"Fifty-Four Forty or Fight"

Democratic slogan, 1844

One year before John O'Sullivan gave the name "Manifest Destiny" to American expansionism (see page 75), the presidential campaign focused on the issue, with Democratic dark horse James Polk of Tennessee supporting the annexation of Texas and the "reoccupation of Oregon," then jointly occupied by the United States and Great Britain. The territory's northern border, expansionists claimed, should be marked above the fifty-fourth parallel—or what today is the southern boundary of Alaska. The Whigs jumped on Polk's obscurity (using "Who is James K. Polk?" as 1988 Democrats used "Who is J. Danforth Quayle?"), but the Tennessean won anyway, and two years after his election he compromised on the Oregon border question: the current U.S.-Canadian border is the forty-ninth parallel he established.

"Free Speech, Free Soil, Free Men, Fremont"

Republican slogan, 1856

In the turbulent debate over slavery that followed the Kansas-Nebraska Act (see page 82), the incumbent Democrats found themselves challenged by two new parties. The Republicans, rallying behind this slogan, demanded the containment of slavery—that is, no expansion into new territories—and the abolition of Mormonism. Members of the American party (from their secretiveness, they were also known as the Know-Nothings) generally wanted slavery in and foreigners out. The Know-Nothings, with former president Millard Fillmore as a candidate, fared poorly on election day but contributed to the victory of Democrat James Buchanan by painting the Republican candidate, Western explorer John Fremont, as both a foreigner *and* a Catholic. The Democrats had charged, more sensibly, that Fremont's election would drive the slaveholding South from the Union; their victory at this time postponed that event by four years.

"Ma, Ma, Where's My Pa?"

Republican song, 1884

The 1884 contest between the Democratic governor of New York, Grover Cleveland, and Pennsylvania's James G. Blaine, was the "mudslingingest" campaign in U.S. history. Blaine, associated with big Eastern money, was charged with "wallowing in spoils like a rhinoceros in an African pool," while his implication in a railroad influence-peddling deal so outraged reform Republicans that they bolted in droves, refusing to support him any longer, to become the Mugwumps. And while Cleveland's public record was impeccable—he campaigned under the slogan "Public Office Is a Public Trust"—he did have a skeleton in his closet: a young woman named Maria Halpin, whose illegitimate child he was supporting. Songwriter H. R. Monroe, in penning the jingle "Ma, Ma, Where's My Pa?" produced a slogan that nearly carried the day until a Blaine supporter, the Rev. Samuel Burchard, called the Democrats the party of "rum, romanism, and rebellion." Blaine's failure to distance himself from this anti-Irish remark helped turn the tide. When Grover the Good was elected, pundits completed the jingle: "Gone to the White House, ha, ha, ha."

"McKinley and the Full Dinner Pail"

Republican slogan, 1896

First prize for oratorical excellence during the 1896 campaign goes to William Jennings Bryan, for his famous "Cross of Gold" speech at the St. Louis Democratic convention. Neither that speech, though, nor his subsequent paeans to Free Silver could get Bryan into the White House. The electorate, deeply divided on the money question (see page 125), was just struggling out of a three-year economic depression. Fearful most of all of instability, the public opted for the gold-standard reassurances of William McKinley, who claimed from his Ohio front porch that "Good money never made times hard." His party's most popular slogan was "McKinley and the Full Dinner Pail." It worked in 1896 and again four years later.

"He Kept Us out of War"

Democratic slogan, 1916

From the beginning of the Great War in 1914 to his reelection campaign two years later, Woodrow Wilson sustained an official, delicate neutrality toward the belligerents Germany and Great Britain, arguing for the protection of civilians from naval attack but refusing, even after the 1915 sinking of the *Lusitania*, to go to war over the loss of American lives. His diplomatic stance, he said in 1915, was "America First"—let frothing Europe stir its own sauce. This equivocating posture provided his party with its 1916 banner—"He Kept Us out of War"—and returned him to the White House by a narrow margin. His Republican opponent, Charles Evans Hughes, tarred by his association with bellicose Teddy Roosevelt (for more on Roosevelt, see page 134), was so given to equivocation himself that he became known as Charles Evasive Hughes. Wilson retook the oath of office in March 1917, and one month later he declared war on Germany.

"Back to Normalcy"

Republican slogan, 1920

The only real issue in the 1920 campaign was U.S. entry into the League of Nations. The Democrats, led by Ohio governor James Cox and his running mate, Franklin Delano Roosevelt, supported it; the Republicans, who offered as running mates Warren Gamaliel Harding and Calvin Coolidge, were opposed. The campaign was largely a referendum on President Wilson's international involvement, with the GOP eventually convincing the public that the country needed a return to simpler times—the days of front-porch swings and honest values and no Great Wars. "Back to Normalcy" was the Republicans' catchy slogan, and nobody seemed to mind that its standard-bearer was a tobacco-chewing, whiskey-sipping womanizer. "Gamaliel"—as writer H. L. Mencken liked to call him—won by about seven million votes.

"A Chicken in Every Pot,
a Car in Every Garage"

Republican boast, 1928

At the end of the sixteenth century, the first Bourbon king, Henri IV, promised his peasants "a chicken in every pot." Three and a half centuries later, in October 1928, the Republican National Committee went him one better, when in a national newspaper ad it announced that Calvin Coolidge's presidency had also put a car in every garage. The moral was to stay the course and vote for Silent Cal's secretary of commerce, Herbert Hoover. An overwhelming majority of Americans did just that, only to be startled into reality one year later, with the onset of the deepest depression in the nation's history.

"Happy Days Are Here Again"

Democratic song, 1932

Although Herbert Hoover was no more responsible for the Great Depression than he had been for the boom that preceded it, Democrats in 1932 gleefully made him the scapegoat, sneered at the "chicken and car" promise, and predicted a return to prosperity under New York's Franklin Delano Roosevelt. The party theme song of that year proclaimed:

> Happy days are here again,
> The skies above are clear again,
> Let's sing a song of cheer again,
> Happy days are here again.

This cheerfully mindless ditty became an unofficial anthem of the New Deal, bringing down the curtain on a dozen years of Republican reign. Although the depression did not lift overnight with the Democrats' takeover of the White House, one aspect of the promised bliss came quickly: the 1933 repeal of Prohibition.

"I Like Ike"

Republican slogan, 1952

Historian Paul Boller cleverly identifies the Republican formula for success in 1952 as K_1C_2—Korea, Communism, and Corruption—and notes how the GOP at the time labeled the Truman administration guilty of "plunder at home, blunder abroad." But the real Republican strength, he observes, lay in unimpeachable Dwight D. Eisenhower, the affable, avuncular farm boy who also happened to be a five-star general. Even the presence of "Tricky Dick" Nixon on the ticket couldn't put voters off, and the "I Like Ike" buttons said it all: voting for Eisenhower was the nice thing to do. Ike beat the equally affable but cripplingly "egghead" Adlai Stevenson by more than six million votes. For the next eight years he charmed his public, and much of the press, with what James Reston called "dynamic platitudes."

"Nixon's the One"

Republican slogan, 1968

In 1962, two years after losing the presidential election to John F. Kennedy and just moments after losing the California gubernatorial race to Pat Brown, the warrior from Whittier promised reporters that they would no longer "have Nixon to kick around." For the next six years he shook hands and bided his time. Then, with the Vietnam War dividing the Democratic party as dramatically as it was dividing the nation, he again became the GOP candidate. With Spiro T. Agnew as his running mate, he watched the Democrats shoot themselves in the foot at their Chicago convention, whipped the law-and-order issue into a lather, and promised to let the Vietnamese fight their own war. Most of the campaign's memorable lines were Agnew gaffes (such as his tagging one reporter a "fat Jap"), but "Nixon's the One" did survive—partly because it was later twisted by liberals into an attack on the Republican's supposed indifference to black America. A couple of years into Nixon's first administration, a poster showed a pregnant black woman pointing to her belly and saying, "Nixon's the one."

"Read My Lips—No New Taxes."

George Bush, 1988

A troubled economy dominated the debates during the 1988 presidential campaign. Democratic candidate Michael Dukakis, flush with raves for his state's economic boom (the so-called Massachusetts Miracle), preached sound management as the way out of a mammoth budget deficit—while endorsing his party's traditional affection for Big Government. Vice-president George Bush, embracing a philosophy whose logic he had once ridiculed as "voodoo economics," claimed the nation could continue on a bloated budget if it would stay the Reagan course of laissez-faire. Bush was endorsing a policy of private initiatives, voluntarism, and "no new taxes." Pressed by reporters on the latter promise, he insisted, "Read my lips—no new taxes." A little more than two years after Bush's election, he signed the tax hike that he said he never would.

Appendix II

In the Heat of Battle

Most of the memorable observations about battle come from such hazardous redoubts as podiums, barstools, and armchairs. That's because ninety-nine times out of a hundred, when a soldier is busy dodging bullets, he doesn't have the presence of mind to come up with a really good catchphrase. There are exceptions. From the ancient world comes Caesar's terse dispatch "I came, I saw, I conquered." From Bosworth Field, according to Shakespeare, comes Richard III's shrill "A horse, a horse, my kingdom for a horse!" And from America come the following history-makers—all uttered with smoke still in the air.

"Don't Fire Until You See the Whites of Their Eyes."

Israel Putnam (1718–1790)

Legend has it that when Israel Putnam heard of the Battle of Lexington and Concord, he stopped plowing a field in midfurrow and rushed off immediately to join the fighting. A prewar leader of the Sons of Liberty and a major general in the Continental Army, "Old Put" uttered his most famous line on June 17, 1775, as redcoats advanced on fortified Breed's Hill in Massachusetts. Evidently the order was followed, for it took the British three tries to dislodge the entrenched Continentals, and they lost more than two hundred men doing so. For reasons known only to military intelligence, this first major engagement of the Revolution became recorded as the Battle of Bunker Hill.

"I Have Not Yet Begun to Fight."

John Paul Jones (1747–1792)

Scottish-born John Paul Jones, privateer in the service of the Stars and Stripes, fought his most memorable battle on September 23, 1779, when his warship, the *Bonhomme Richard*, engaged the British frigate *Serapis* in English waters. When a British victory seemed assured, the *Serapis*'s captain, Richard Pearson, called for Jones's surrender. Jones's reply proved more than a boast, for at the end of the three-hour battle it was Pearson whose colors were struck. Jones transferred his command to the defeated vessel, cut his devastated flagship adrift to sink, and became a demigod to the fledgling U.S. Navy. After the war he worked for the Russian Navy, becoming a rear admiral under Catherine the Great.

"Don't Give Up the Ship."

James Lawrence (1781–1813)

James Lawrence, captain of the USS *Chesapeake* in the War of 1812, was as hardy in spirit as his predecessor, Jones, but not quite so lucky. On June 1, 1813, while engaging the British warship *Shannon* offshore from Boston, he was wounded mortally and carried below decks as a boarding party prepared to take his ship. Dying, he ordered his crew to scuttle her—his last words in full were "Don't give up the ship! Sink her! Blow her up!"—but to no avail. Battle, captain, and craft were all lost.

"We Have Met the Enemy, and They Are Ours."

Oliver Hazard Perry (1785–1819)

The elder brother of Commodore Matthew Perry, who opened U.S. trade with Japan, Oliver Hazard Perry commanded the American fleet at the decisive Battle of Lake Erie (September 10, 1813), which gave the United States control of the Great Lakes area and got from the British its first fleet surrender in history. Perry's laconic report to nearby ground commander William Henry Harrison (the hero of

Tippecanoe, see page 43) ranks right up there with Julius Caesar's *"Veni, vidi, vici"* and the comment of World War II flyer David Mason on his destruction of a Japanese submarine: "Sighted sub. Sank same." Nationally lionized after the war, Perry was rewarded with a diplomatic mission to Latin America, where he contracted the yellow fever that ended his life.

"There Stands Jackson Like a Stone Wall."
Barnard Bee (1823–1861)

The first major battle of the Civil War took place near Manassas, Virginia, on July 21, 1861. In this First Battle of Bull Run, the Union's expectation of an easy victory, and thus a quick war, was thwarted largely by an indomitable Southern line commanded by Bible-quoting Thomas Jonathan Jackson. When fellow Confederate general Barnard Bee observed Jackson's tenacity, he unwittingly gave him a nickname that Jackson would carry until his death by "friendly fire" at Chancellorsville, Virginia, two years later. Bee himself did not survive Bull Run.

"Damn the Torpodeos! Full Speed Ahead!"
David G. Farragut (1801–1870)

A teenage veteran of the War of 1812, David G. Farragut had to wait almost forty years after receiving his first command before he would find the battle that gave him his fame. Instructed in 1864 to take the port of Mobile, Alabama, from the Confederacy, Farragut moved his fleet into Mobile Bay on August 5 and almost immediately lost an ironclad warship to a mine—then called a "torpedo." Undaunted, he climbed the rigging of his flagship, bellowed out his famous curse, and three hours later secured the port for the Union. At the war's end, at the age of sixty-six, he became the country's first admiral.

"Fire When Ready, Gridley."

George Dewey (1837–1917)

Barely one week after the declaration of war on Spain, U.S. Asiatic Squadron commander George Dewey, acting on orders from President Theodore Roosevelt, sailed into the Philippines' Manila Bay and, in a dawn attack on May 1, 1898, reduced the Spanish fleet to twisted rubble. The order that began the attack, which was given to flagship commander Charles Vernon Gridley, actually ran, "You may fire when you are ready, Gridley." Acclaimed as a war hero, Dewey was briefly considered presidential timber, became the nation's first five-star admiral, and headed the navy's general board until his death.

"Praise the Lord and Pass the Ammunition."

Howell M. Forgy (1908–)

Howell M. Forgy was a U.S. Navy chaplain stationed to the cruiser *New Orleans* in Pearl Harbor when, on December 7, 1941, Japanese planes started the "date which will live in infamy." As a man of the cloth, Forgy could not man the guns himself, but he did shout a celebrated line of encouragement. A perfect blend of piety and practicality, it soon became an armed-forces slogan, and in 1942 a popular song.

"Nuts!"

Anthony C. McAuliffe (1898–1975)

On December 22, 1944, Anthony C. McAuliffe commanded the 101st Airborne Division in a defense of Bastogne, Belgium, against a German advance during the Battle of the Bulge. Upon demanding surrender, the German commander met with McAuliffe's one-word reply. Not as elegant as John Paul Jones's, maybe, but it got the idea across. Bastogne never was surrendered, and, as a result, McAuliffe became a major general.

Appendix III

The Dirty Dozen

In college we called them "gobbets": quickie definitions of lesser pieces in the historical puzzle. You didn't need them to understand the Big Picture, but having them made you secure (or at least made you *feel* secure) when confronted by pedants. European gobbets included identification of things like "Roncesvalles" and "We will not go to Canossa." An American sampling might include the following dozen.

1. **Barnburners.** Antislavery Democrats who, in 1848, left to join the Free Soil party, which opposed extension of the "peculiar institution." They were said to endorse "burning down the barn" (of the Democratic party) in order to get rid of its pro-slavery "rats."

2. **Victoria and Tennessee Claflin.** Spiritualist sisters turned pioneering feminists. Their newsletter charged Henry Ward Beecher (brother of Harriet Beecher Stowe) with adultery. Running on the Equal Rights ticket, "Vicky" lost the 1872 presidential race to U. S. Grant.

3. **Father Coughlin.** Charles Coughlin, a fervently anti-Roosevelt Roman Catholic priest whose Detroit radio show in the 1930s lambasted, among other things, Communism, the New Deal, and Jewish money. At the height of his popularity the "Radio Priest" employed more than a hundred assistants to handle his mail.

4. **Deep Throat.** The unidentified source who provided Bob Woodward and Carl Bernstein with damning evidence against the Nixon administration in their 1973 Watergate investigation. Named for a popular pornographic movie of the time.

5. **Embalmed Beef.** A Spanish-American War scandal, involving charges that canned army rations had been tainted with "experimen-

tal" preservatives. An investigation demanded by Teddy Roosevelt proved inconclusive.

6. **Gadsden Purchase.** A thirty-thousand-square-mile tract of land bought from Mexico for a railroad right-of-way in 1853. Named for rail tycoon James Gadsden, it now forms the border counties of Arizona and New Mexico.

7. **The Hair Buyer.** Nickname of Detroit's British governor, Henry Hamilton, during the American Revolution. From his practice (not uncommon in this period) of paying his Indian allies for rebel American scalps.

8. **Knights of the Golden Horseshoe.** The most famous Northern proslavery, or "Copperhead," organization during the Civil War. In 1864, paying a curious homage to the colonial period's patriot radicals, it changed its name to the Sons of Liberty.

9. **Lemonade Lucy.** President Rutherford B. Hayes's teetotaling wife, the former Lucy Ware Webb. The first college-educated First Lady, she banned alcoholic beverages from the White House and also started the tradition of the annual Easter-egg roll on the residence's lawn.

10. **Rappites.** Followers of Protestant reformer George Rapp, founder of one of the nineteenth century's most successful utopian projects, the Harmony Society. After establishing communities in Pennsylvania and Indiana, the society survived, communistic and officially celibate, for almost a century.

11. **Tennis Cabinet.** Popular epithet for President Teddy Roosevelt's tennis-playing cronies, who formed an unofficial cabinet in his administration. Not to be confused with President Andrew Jackson's unofficial advisers, commonly referred to as the Kitchen Cabinet.

12. **Whispering Campaign.** The word-of-mouth anti-Catholic innuendo that helped defeat Democratic (and Catholic) presidential candidate Al Smith in 1928. Fears of papal influence over the White House were fanned by, among others, the Ku Klux Klan.

Index

abolitionists, 74, 80, 85–85, 89–93
Acheson, Dean, 184
Adams, John, 17, 32, 47, 63, 65
Adams, John Quincy, 58–59, 61
Adams, Samuel, 16, 18, 22
African-Americans, 17, 31, 101, 189.
 See also civil rights, slavery.
Agnew, Spiro, 205–7, 226
Alamo, 67–68
Albany Regency, 65
alcohol, 13, 36, 41, 104, 149–51, 233
Alden, John, 9, 22
Alien and Sedition Acts, 29
"All men are created equal," 30, 95
Alliance for Progress, 188
alphabet agencies, 161–63. See also
 New Deal.
Altgeld, John Peter, 117
Amendments, Constitutional, 44–46,
 59, 73, 94, 101, 103, 110, 138–39,
 147, 150
American Civil Liberties Union
 (ACLU), 44, 123, 151, 155, 217
American Expeditionary Forces, 143
American Federation of Labor (AFL),
 118
America First Committee, 170
American party, 115, 222
American System, 60
anarchists, 116–17, 153–55
Andre, John, 33
Anthony, Susan B., 147
anticommunism, 153–55, 182–84, 188,
 215, 232
Anti-Federalists, 41, 44, 46. See also
 Federalists, states' rights.
antitrust laws, 98, 118, 121, 132
Appomattox Court House, 99
Armstrong, Neil, 205
Arnold, Benedict, 33, 100
"arsenal of democracy," 168–70
Articles of Confederation, 39
"Ask not what your country can do for
 you," 186

Atlantic Charter, 170
Attucks, Crispus, 16
Austin, Stephen F., 67

Babcock, Orville, 104
baby boom, 180
banks, 46, 64, 157–58, 162
Barbary Coast, 55–56
Barnburners, 232
"Battle Hymn of the Republic," 91
Bay of Pigs, 136, 187
beaver, 11
Bee, Barnard, 230
Beecher, Henry Ward, 83, 90, 232
Bell, Alexander Bell, 105
Bellamy, Edward, 136
Berlin Wall, 177, 187, 189
Biddle, Nicholas, 65
big stick, 58, 134–36
Big Red Scare, 154
Bill of Rights, 21, 44–46
black codes, 101
Black Friday, 104
Black Hills, 78, 107
Black Muslims, 200–201
Black Panthers, 191, 200–203
Black Power, 200
Black Tuesday, 157
Blaine, James G., 223
"Bleeding Kansas," 81, 90
Boland Amendment, 214
bomb, nuclear, 175, 181, 182, 188, 192
"Bomb them back into the Stone Age,"
 180
Bonus Army, 178
Booth, John Wilkes, 99–100
Border Ruffians, 82
Boston Massacre, 15, 23
Boston Tea Party, 17, 23
Bowie, James, 67–68
Boxer Rebellion, 131
Braddock's Defeat, 11
Bradford, William, 8
brain trust, 139, 163

About the Author

Born in New Jersey in 1944, Tad Tuleja earned a B.A. (magna cum laude) in European cultural history from Yale University and an M.A. in American Studies from the University of Sussex. He has been a college writing instructor, journalist, editor, and encyclopedia researcher as well as the author (or coauthor) of twenty-five books. His several reference works include books on word lore, popular beliefs, and social customs. A member of the American Folklore Society and the American Studies Association, Tuleja lives with his wife and daughter in Austin, Texas, where he is doing graduate work in folklore and anthropology.